PAT BROWN, MBA

BasketballMoney101

Using Basketball to Teach the Basics of Money

AF808691

ABRAM 47 BROWN

First published by AbramBrown47 2026

First edition

ISBN: 978-1-967737-49-9

This book was professionally typeset on Reedsy.
Find out more at reedsy.com

Contents

Foreword

Basketball teaches you lessons long before anyone calls them life skills.

You learn how to show up early and stay late.

You learn that talent gets attention, but habits determine minutes.

You learn that one bad possession does not define you, but how you respond to it does.

You learn that the game rewards discipline, patience, and preparation far more than flash.

What basketball does not teach you is what happens **after the final buzzer**.

When the season ends, the structure disappears. There is no practice schedule. No film session. No coach setting expectations. No clear scoreboard telling you how you are doing. For many former student-athletes, that silence is louder than any crowd they ever played in front of.

This is where money quietly becomes a problem.

Not because athletes are irresponsible.

Not because they lack intelligence.

But because the same structure that helped them succeed on the court no longer exists off it.

Basketball players are trained to compete under pressure. They understand reps, game plans, roles, and long-term development. What they are rarely given is a financial playbook that speaks the same language. Instead, they are expected to figure it out on their own. Learn taxes by making mistakes. Learn budgeting by falling behind. Learn investing by listening to the loudest voice in the room.

That approach would never work in basketball. It does not work with money either.

Basketball Money 101 exists to close that gap.

This book does not try to turn you into a finance expert. It does not promise shortcuts, hot tips, or overnight wins. What it does is translate the fundamentals you already understand into a system you can use in real life. Preparation becomes planning. Film study becomes awareness. Discipline becomes consistency. Team basketball becomes diversification. Halftime adjustments become long-term decision-making.

If you ever learned to run an offense, you can learn to manage cash flow.

If you ever trusted a game plan, you can trust a long-term financial strategy.

If you ever stayed locked in when shots were not falling, you can stay disciplined when markets are volatile.

The athletes who struggle after sports are not the ones who lack work ethic. They are the ones who lose structure. This book helps you rebuild it.

Basketball may end.

Your financial life does not.

Winning off the court does not require perfection. It requires fundamentals, patience, and the willingness to keep showing up when no one is watching.

This book is your playbook for that next season.

Read it the way you would watch film.

Apply it the way you would execute a game plan.

Respect the fundamentals.

And trust that consistency still wins.

The buzzer has sounded.

The next possession is yours.

Introduction

Every basketball player understands the shot clock.

You feel it even when you are not looking at it.

The pace changes. Decisions speed up. Good shots matter more. Bad ones get exposed faster.

You do not need to be told time is running out. You sense it.

Life does not have a shot clock hanging above it.

There is no buzzer warning you that a season is ending. No horn telling you a window is closing. No official stopping play and handing you a reset. From the outside, that sounds freeing. In reality, it is why so many people drift.

For athletes, that drift can be dangerous.

Basketball trains you to operate inside structure. Practice schedules. Game plans. Film sessions. Roles. Accountability. Someone is always tracking minutes, effort, and execution. When the final buzzer sounds for the last time, that structure disappears overnight. Suddenly, time is wide open. Decisions are optional. Discipline becomes self-directed.

And money shows up right in the middle of that transition.

Not all at once. Not dramatically. Quietly.

A paycheck here. A bill there. A credit card. A lifestyle upgrade. A decision you will deal with later. Without a shot clock, it feels like there is always more time. More time to save. More time to learn. More time to clean things up.

There usually is not.

Time is still the most important factor in money, even when no one is counting it down for you. The difference is that in life, time works in the background. It rewards consistency and punishes delay without ever making noise.

Basketball players already understand this concept better than most.

You know that missing offseason work shows up months later. You know that bad habits compound. You know that the players who last are not always the most talented, but the most disciplined. Those same truths apply to money. The only difference is that the feedback loop is slower and the consequences arrive quietly.

This is where mistakes happen.

Former student-athletes do not fail financially because they stop caring. They fail because there is no game plan for what comes next. They rely on instincts. They chase momentum. They trust confidence over preparation. That works on the court. Off the court, it leads to forced shots.

This book exists to slow the game down.

Basketball Money 101 is not about urgency or panic. It is about awareness. It is about understanding how time, discipline, and structure shape financial outcomes long after basketball ends. You will not find hype or shortcuts here. You will find fundamentals explained in a language you already speak.

If you can manage the clock in a close game, you can manage cash flow.

If you can trust a system during a shooting slump, you can stay disciplined through financial uncertainty.

If you can adjust at halftime, you can adjust when life changes.

There is no shot clock on life, but every decision still takes time off the board.

The players who win long term are not the ones who rush. They are the ones who stay intentional, protect their future possessions, and make smart decisions possession by possession.

Basketball may be over.

The season that follows is longer.

This book is designed to help you play it well.

About This Book

This book is not meant to be read like a finance textbook.

It is meant to be used the way you learned basketball. Through fundamentals, repetition, discipline, and clear expectations. Basketball players do not learn by memorizing theory. They learn by running drills, watching film, making mistakes, and adjusting. That is exactly how this book is built.

Basketball and money operate on the same principles.

Both reward preparation long before results show up.

Both punish emotional decisions made under pressure.

Both favor players who stay disciplined when things are not going their way.

Both are won possession by possession, not with one highlight play.

The problem is not that athletes lack the ability to manage money. The problem is that money is rarely taught in a way that matches how athletes actually think and learn. Most financial advice is abstract. It relies on jargon, formulas, and long explanations disconnected from real decision-making. Basketball players live in a world of spacing, timing, roles, and execution. When money is taught without that context, it feels foreign.

This book connects the dots.

Every financial concept in *Basketball Money 101* is explained through basketball fundamentals you already understand. Budgeting is treated like running an offense. Saving is built through repetition, not willpower. Risk management mirrors defensive awareness. Investing is about shot selection, spacing, and patience, not constant movement. Long-term planning is about managing the season, not forcing plays early.

You will see basketball language throughout the book because it matters. Concepts stick when they are framed in familiar terms. When you understand why a financial decision works the same way a basketball decision works, it becomes easier to execute under pressure.

Each chapter follows a consistent structure.

You will start with a basketball scenario that feels real. A moment in practice, a game situation, a decision under pressure. From there, the financial concept is explained by directly mapping it to how basketball works. Nothing abstract. Nothing theoretical. The goal is clarity, not complexity.

You will also see guidance framed the way a coach would deliver it. Direct. Honest. Focused on habits and accountability. Coaches do not sugarcoat mistakes, and neither does this book. Discipline, consistency, and fundamentals are emphasized because they hold up when emotions run high.

At the end of each chapter, you will find a short section called *Athlete Takeaways*. These are not summaries. They are reminders. Simple points written in basketball language that you can apply immediately to real-life decisions.

You do not need to read this book cover to cover in one sitting. Just like a playbook, some sections will matter more to you right now than others. You can jump to the chapter that fits your current situation, or you can read it from start to finish and build your foundation the right way. The progression is intentional, but the application is flexible.

This book will not promise financial success.

Basketball never promised wins either.

What it will give you is a system. A way to think about money that matches how you already think about preparation, reps, adjustments, and long-term development. Winning financially does not require brilliance. It requires discipline applied consistently over time.

You already know how to do that.

This book shows you how to translate it off the court.

Foolish Assumptions

Every good coach starts with assumptions.

Not because they believe every player is the same, but because a system only works when there is a shared baseline. Expectations matter. Roles matter. Accountability matters. This book is no different.

In *Basketball Money 101,* these assumptions are called **foolish** not because they are careless, but because they are honest. They may not fit everyone perfectly, but they fit well enough to build something that works.

Here is what this book assumes about you.

It assumes you understand discipline.

You have shown up early and stayed late. You have run drills when no one was watching. You know that talent gets you noticed, but habits keep you on the floor. You understand that effort is not optional, and that shortcuts eventually get exposed.

It assumes you have been coached hard.

You have been corrected. You have been challenged. You have heard things you did not want to hear and learned to respond instead of react. You understand that feedback is not personal. It is part of growth. You know the difference between being attacked and being held accountable.

It assumes you understand preparation.

You know that games are not won at tipoff. They are won in practice, in the weight room, and in film sessions. You understand that consistency beats intensity and that preparation creates confidence when pressure rises.

It assumes you are competitive.

You care about outcomes. You want to improve. You do not like feeling behind. Even if you are no longer playing, that edge is still there. This book assumes you want to win, not just survive.

It assumes you are not a financial expert.

You may know some things. You may have picked up advice along the way. But no one handed you a structured financial education designed for how athletes think and learn. That is not a failure. That is reality.

It assumes you have made mistakes or will make some.

Every player misses shots. Every player blows assignments. Money is no different. This book assumes you are willing to learn, adjust, and keep moving forward rather than pretending mistakes did not happen.

It assumes you are willing to take responsibility.

Not for everything that has happened to you, but for what happens next. Basketball teaches ownership. This book expects the same. Blaming the refs never changed the score. Avoiding responsibility never fixes financial problems.

It assumes you want something beyond short-term wins.

You want stability. You want options. You want to build something that lasts beyond one season or one paycheck. You want to make decisions today that do not limit you tomorrow.

If these assumptions feel fair, this book will work for you.

If you are looking for shortcuts, guarantees, or someone else to manage everything for you without effort, this is not the right playbook.

Basketball rewards players who do the work.

Money works the same way.

These assumptions are the foundation. Everything that follows is built on them.

How This Playbook Is Organized

This book is organized the same way a basketball season is played.

You do not start the season running complex sets.

You do not skip conditioning.

You do not worry about the scoreboard before you understand spacing, roles, and fundamentals.

Everything builds in the right order.

Basketball Money 101 is structured into clear parts, each one designed to mirror how basketball actually works and how financial decisions unfold over time. The goal is not to overwhelm you. The goal is to build confidence through progression.

Part I: Mastering the Fundamentals (Preseason Work)

This is where everything starts.

Before minutes, before stats, before outcomes, there is preparation. In this section, you build your financial foundation the same way you built your basketball foundation. You learn how money flows in and out of your life, how to read your own box score, and how to run a basic financial offense without forcing shots.

Nothing flashy. Just the fundamentals that make everything else possible.

If you skip this part, you will spend the rest of your financial life playing from behind.

Part II: Defense, Protection, and Staying in the Game

Great teams protect the paint, communicate, and avoid unnecessary fouls.

This section focuses on financial defense. Risk awareness, insurance, and protection are not about fear. They are about staying available. One bad hit, one lawsuit, one unexpected event can undo years of effort if you are unprepared.

Defense does not win headlines, but it keeps you on the floor long enough to win.

Part III: Scoring With Purpose (Investing Fundamentals)

This is where you learn how to score without forcing the game.

Investing is not about heat checks or highlight plays. It is about shot selection, spacing, and patience. In this section, you learn how markets work, what you actually own when you invest, and how discipline over time creates results.

Smart offenses take what the defense gives them. Smart investors do the same.

Part IV: Managing the Season (Portfolio Management)

No season goes exactly as planned.

Roles change. Injuries happen. Life does the same thing to your finances. This section teaches you how to review, adjust, and stay disciplined without overreacting. Rebalancing, reviewing progress, and making smart halftime adjustments are how you stay competitive over long seasons.

This is where maturity shows up.

Part V: The Long Season (Taxes, Family, and Life Stages)

Basketball ends. Your financial life does not.

This section addresses the realities that show up after the uniform comes off. Taxes, housing, careers, family responsibilities, and long-term planning all live here. These decisions rarely feel urgent, but they shape your future more than any single investment.

This is where short-term thinking quietly does the most damage.

Part VI: Winning Beyond the Scoreboard

This final section focuses on leadership and accountability.

Knowing when to ask for help. Understanding how advisors work. Avoiding scams and bad advice. Learning from mistakes and staying focused on long-term success. Winning beyond the scoreboard is about playing the long game with intention.

Part VII: Life After the Final Buzzer

The last section brings everything together.

This is about identity, structure, and discipline when no one is setting the schedule for you. It addresses the real-world transition former student-athletes face and shows how to rebuild systems that support growth long after basketball ends.

Each chapter follows the same rhythm.

A basketball scenario you will recognize.

A clear financial lesson mapped directly to the game.

Coach-style guidance focused on discipline and fundamentals.

Real decision points that mirror life off the court.

And a short set of *Athlete Takeaways* you can apply immediately.

You can read this book straight through or jump to the sections that matter most right now. Just like a playbook, not every page is needed in every moment.

But the order matters if you want the full benefit.
Start with the fundamentals.
Protect what you build.
Score with purpose.
Adjust when needed.
And think long term.
That is how basketball works.
That is how money works.

About Pat Brown

Pat Brown played college football at the University of Kansas from 1994 to 1999 and was named team captain for the 1999 season. His years in the locker room shaped his views on accountability, discipline, preparation, and leadership, principles that continue to guide his work long after football.

Following his playing career, Pat transitioned into financial services and built a career as a financial advisor and wealth manager. He works with individuals, families, business owners, and athletes navigating increasingly complex financial lives. He pursued advanced education and professional development, earning an MBA along with industry designations including ChFC®, RICP®, and CAP®. His background blends academic training with real-world experience in financial planning, retirement income strategies, tax planning, and philanthropy.

As the college sports landscape changed with the introduction of Name, Image, and Likeness opportunities, Pat recognized a growing education gap. Student athletes were gaining access to income, contracts, and endorsements without the financial knowledge needed to manage taxes, cash flow, business structures, and long-term consequences. That reality became the catalyst for his work in the NIL space.

Pat has since become a recognized voice in athlete financial education and has been interviewed by national publications and platforms including Financial Planning, Yahoo, and ESPN Andscape, where he shares insights on NIL planning, financial literacy gaps, and the challenges facing student athletes and their families.

These experiences led Pat to author a series of practical, athlete-focused books designed to meet athletes and families where they are. His NIL-related titles include *Financial Literacy for NIL, Financial Literacy for NIL for Parents of Student Athletes, Financial Literacy for NIL for High School Students,* and *Financial Literacy for NIL for International Student Athletes.* Each book is written to be clear, accessible, and grounded in real-world scenarios rather than theory.

Pat also created a growing collection of sport-specific financial education titles, including *Football Money 101, Baseball Money 101, Basketball Money 101, Cheer Money 101, Dance Money 101, Gymnastics Money 101, Hockey Money 101, Lacrosse Money 101, Rowing Money 101, Soccer Money 101, Softball Money 101, Tennis Money 101, Track Money 101, Volleyball Money 101,* and *Wrestling Money 101.* Each book translates the culture, discipline, and mindset of the sport into financial lessons athletes can apply long after competition ends.

To extend this mission beyond books, Pat founded Former Student Athlete, a platform created to support athletes navigating life after sports. Former Student Athlete provides education, community, and real-world resources focused on financial literacy, career transitions, health, identity, and long-term success once the uniform comes off. His broader education platforms can be found at www.formerstudentathlete.com, www.financialliteracyfornil.com, www.financialliteracyforstudentathletes.com, and www.parentsofstudentathletes.com.

Pat is easy to find through a Google search, on LinkedIn, or on Twitter, where he regularly shares insights on athletes, money, and life after sports. If you would like to visit with Pat specifically about Basketball *Money 101,* you can reach him directly at info@basketballmoney101.com.

Pat's work is rooted in a belief shaped by both football and finance. Athletes deserve a better playbook for life after sports, and financial education should arrive before opportunity turns into regret.

Part I: Mastering the Fundamentals (Preseason Work)

Great players do not skip fundamentals. Neither do great financial decisions.

Every basketball season starts the same way.

Not with packed gyms, highlight plays, or pressure possessions, but with work that rarely gets attention. Conditioning. Footwork. Shooting form. Defensive slides. Reps that feel repetitive and unglamorous. Coaches insist on this phase because they know something players sometimes forget. Games are won long before tipoff.

Money works the same way.

Most financial mistakes are not caused by complex situations or bad luck. They come from skipping the preseason. From trying to make plays without understanding spacing. From forcing shots without knowing the system. From wanting results before building habits.

Athletes would never expect to walk onto the court without learning the basics. Yet many are forced to approach money exactly that way. Income shows up before education. Decisions appear without context. Mistakes get made quietly and compound over time.

This section is about building your financial foundation the same way you built your basketball foundation.

You will not find advanced strategies here. You will not find hype or shortcuts. What you will find are the fundamentals that support everything else. Understanding how money moves in and out of your life. Learning how to read your own box score. Building systems that create consistency without relying on motivation.

Preseason work is not exciting, but it is essential.

This is where habits are formed.

This is where discipline is tested.

This is where confidence is built before pressure shows up.

If you get this part right, the rest of the game slows down. Decisions become clearer. Mistakes become easier to correct. Progress becomes sustainable.

If you skip it, you spend the season playing catch-up.

Mastering the fundamentals does not guarantee success. Basketball never made that promise either. What it does is put you in position to compete possession by possession, no matter what the season throws at you.

This is the work.

This is the foundation.

This is where winning starts.

Chapter 1: Why Money Feels Confusing After the Final Buzzer

Think back to your first real game.

Not the scrimmage. Not open gym. The first game that counted.

The speed felt different. The reads were faster. Help defense arrived sooner than expected. Passing windows closed quicker. The margin for error shrank instantly. Even things you had practiced thousands of times suddenly felt unfamiliar once the lights came on.

It was not because you were unprepared.

It was because experience changes how information shows up.

Basketball feels simple when you understand it. Before that, it feels chaotic.

Money works the same way.

Most athletes do not struggle with money because they are careless, lazy, or irresponsible. They struggle because they are thrown into real financial decisions without a system, without reps, and without coaching.

One day basketball provides structure for nearly every hour of your life. Wake-up times. Training. Film. Practice. Study hall. Travel. Meals. Recovery. Someone else has thought through the framework so you can focus on execution.

Then the final buzzer sounds.

Suddenly, you are expected to manage income, expenses, credit, savings, investing, taxes, and long-term decisions on your own.

No walkthroughs.

No film session.

No playbook.

That is why money feels confusing.

Why Financial Literacy Is Rarely Taught to Athletes

Athletes grow up inside structure.

Schedules are set. Paperwork is handled. Meals appear. Travel is planned. Gear is provided. Even housing and healthcare are often managed for you. This is not a flaw in the system. It is how high-performance environments work. The goal is to remove distractions so you can train, compete, and recover.

The problem shows up when that structure disappears.

Financial education is often treated as someone else's responsibility.

Schools assume families will teach it.

Families assume athletes will learn later.

Teams focus on performance, not paychecks.

By the time real money shows up, the education is already late.

Basketball teaches you how to read defenses, manage pace, and adjust under pressure. It rarely teaches you how to read a bank statement, manage credit, or plan beyond the next season.

So when income changes, expenses increase, or decisions stack up, athletes feel behind. Not because they are incapable, but because they were never trained for this part of the game.

You cannot execute what you were never taught.

Money Myths Passed Through Locker Rooms and AAU Circuits

Every locker room has money talk.

Someone knows a player who "made it big" in crypto.

Someone else claims the stock market is gambling.

Someone swears debt is always bad.

Someone else says debt does not matter if you make enough.

The loudest voice usually sounds the most confident, and confidence spreads fast in athletic environments.

Common myths sound like this:

If you are not investing, you are falling behind.

Being aggressive always wins.

Saving is for people who do not make enough.

Debt is either dangerous or free money.

These ideas stick because they are simple and emotional. They also collapse under pressure.

Basketball does not operate on myths. You would never change your shooting form because someone said it worked for them once. You would never adopt a defensive scheme because a teammate "felt good about it." You demand film, reps, and proof.

Money deserves the same discipline.

Most financial mistakes athletes make are not intelligence problems. They are noise problems.

Saving vs Investing vs Gambling

This confusion causes more damage than almost anything else.

Saving, investing, and gambling are not the same thing, even though people talk about them as if they are.

Saving is about protection.

It is money you can access quickly. Emergency funds. Short-term needs. Stability. Saving keeps small problems from becoming big ones.

Investing is about ownership and growth over time.

It requires patience. Ups and downs are normal. Results come from staying in the system, not from perfect timing.

Gambling is chasing outcomes without a plan.

No protection. No margin for error. Emotion-driven decisions. Wins feel exciting. Losses are ignored until they compound.

In basketball terms, saving is conditioning. It does not win games directly, but without it you break down late.

Investing is running the offense. You trust spacing, timing, and execution.

Gambling is forcing a contested shot early in the clock and hoping it goes in.

Many athletes skip saving because it feels slow. They jump straight to investing or speculation. That is like skipping warmups and expecting to play heavy minutes without consequences.

It works until it does not.

Why Consistency Beats Highlight Plays

Basketball rewards players who do the small things well every day.

Same shooting form.

Same defensive stance.

Same preparation.

Highlights come and go. Consistency keeps you on the floor.

Money works the same way.

You do not need the perfect budget. You need a simple one you can actually follow.

You do not need the perfect investment strategy. You need discipline over time.

You do not need to know everything. You need to start and keep showing up.

Consistency builds confidence.

Confidence builds discipline.

Discipline builds results.

Athletes who win financially are not chasing big wins. They are protecting their base, managing risk, and stacking good decisions.

Just like basketball, fundamentals separate professionals from highlight chasers.

Why Experience Changes Everything

At first, basketball feels fast because you are reacting.

Later, it slows down because you anticipate.

Money is the same.

Early on, bills feel stressful. Decisions feel overwhelming. Choices feel permanent. Over time, systems replace emotion. Structure replaces guesswork. The game slows down.

The goal is not perfection.

The goal is composure.

Coach's Perspective

If a coach were talking about money, the message would sound familiar.

Do your job.

Make the simple play.

Control what you can control.

We do not take possessions off.

Money does not need heroics. It needs fundamentals. Fundamentals hold up under pressure. That is why coaches never stop teaching them, even to veterans.

Game Situations and Decision Points

You get your first real paycheck.

Do you spend first and hope there is something left, or protect part of it immediately?

You hear about a hot opportunity.

Do you chase it without understanding, or stick to a plan you can execute?

You realize you have no emergency fund.

Do you ignore it and hope nothing happens, or start building protection now?

Just like basketball, the moment matters less than the decision.

Common Athlete Mistakes and Financial Parallels

Athletes get impatient.

Financially, that shows up as chasing quick wins.

Athletes trust confidence over preparation.

Financially, that shows up as following bad advice.

Athletes hate feeling behind.

Financially, that leads to forcing decisions.

The same mistakes that lose games lose money.

Winning the Long Game

Basketball careers are short. Financial lives are long.

You do not need to win today. You need to stay in the game. Progress beats perfection. The players who succeed long after the final buzzer are the ones who treat money like a season, not a single possession.

You build momentum by showing up, running the system, and stacking good days.

Athlete Takeaways

Do not skip the preseason. Fundamentals come before flash.

Saving protects you. Investing grows you. Gambling guesses.

Loud locker room advice is not a game plan.

Consistency beats highlight plays.

Stay disciplined and stack good possessions.

This is how the game slows down.

Chapter 2: Know the Box Score: Your Financial Snapshot

Every basketball player knows the box score matters.

You might remember one great play, a tough defensive stop, or one bad miss that still bothers you. But the box score tells the full story. Minutes played. Points scored. Assists. Turnovers. Fouls. Rebounds. Efficiency. It does not care how you felt about the game. It does not care what almost happened. It shows what actually happened.

That is why coaches start there.

Before adjustments. Before praise. Before criticism. The box score and the film come first.

Money has a box score too.

Most former student-athletes avoid it. Not because they are irresponsible, but because no one ever taught them how to read it. Bank balances feel scattered. Bills hit at different times. Spending happens automatically. Subscriptions run quietly in the background. Instead of checking the numbers, people rely on gut feel.

"I think I'm fine."

"I feel like I should have more."

"I don't know where it's going, but it's working… I think."

That is how small problems turn into big ones.

Just like basketball, if you do not know the score, you cannot make adjustments.

Before you change anything, you need to know the score.

Income, Expenses, and Cash Flow

Cash flow is how money moves through your life.

Income is what comes in.

Paychecks. Bonuses. Side work. NIL income for some athletes.

Expenses are what go out.

Rent. Food. Transportation. Subscriptions. Training costs. Lifestyle spending.

Cash flow is the difference between the two.

In basketball terms, income is points scored. Expenses are points allowed. Cash flow tells you whether you are winning the game or slowly digging yourself into a hole.

A lot of athletes focus only on income. More money feels like progress. A raise feels like winning. A bigger check feels like security.

But if spending rises just as fast, nothing actually improves.

You can score 30 points and still lose if you give up 35.

Positive cash flow gives you options.

Negative cash flow puts you under pressure.

When cash flow is positive, you can save, invest, and absorb mistakes. When cash flow is negative, everything feels urgent. Stress increases. Credit gets used. Decisions get rushed.

You do not need complicated spreadsheets or advanced software to understand cash flow. You need awareness.

Know what comes in.

Know what goes out.

Everything else builds from there.

Assets, Liabilities, and Net Worth

Assets are things you own that have value.

Cash.

Investments.

Property.

Businesses.

Liabilities are what you owe.

Credit cards.

Student loans.

Car loans.

Mortgages.

Net worth is the difference between the two.

In basketball terms, assets are your strengths. Liabilities are vulnerabilities. Net worth is the overall matchup.

One strong asset does not cancel out multiple weaknesses. Just like one elite scorer does not fix poor defense, low effort, or constant turnovers. You have to look at the whole picture.

Many athletes confuse income with wealth.

Income is what you earn.

Net worth is what you keep and build over time.

You can make good money and still be fragile financially if liabilities keep growing. You can make modest income and still build strength if assets grow consistently.

The box score does not care about potential. It cares about results.

Fixed vs Variable Expenses

Not all expenses are the same.

Fixed expenses stay mostly consistent.

Rent. Insurance. Loan payments. Phone plans.

Variable expenses change month to month.

Food. Travel. Entertainment. Convenience spending. Subscriptions.

Fixed expenses are like your base defense. They define your structure. Once they are set, they are harder to move quickly.

Variable expenses are where adjustments happen.

Most people try to cut big fixed costs first, which is often difficult and frustrating. The real leverage is usually in variable spending you barely notice.

Coffee stops.

Food delivery.

Streaming services.

Impulse purchases.

Each one feels small. Over a season, they add up.

In basketball, missed box-outs and lazy closeouts do not always show up immediately. Over time, they cost games. Money works the same way.

Little leaks add up over a season.

Film Study on Where Your Money Actually Goes

This is the most uncomfortable part, and the most important.

Pull your bank statements.

Pull your credit card statements.

Look at them honestly.

No judgment.

No excuses.

Just facts.

Film study is not punishment. It is improvement.

You are not looking for perfection. You are looking for patterns.

You might notice:

Subscriptions you forgot about.

Convenience spending that adds up faster than expected.

Lifestyle choices that do not match what you say matters to you.

This is not about shame. Coaches do not show film to embarrass players. They show it to create clarity.

If you do not watch the film, you keep repeating the same mistakes.

The numbers are not there to criticize you. They are there to help you get better.

Why Athletes Avoid the Box Score

Athletes avoid the financial box score for the same reason players avoid bad film.

It threatens identity.

It creates discomfort.

It forces accountability.

But avoiding it does not improve performance.

In basketball, confidence comes from preparation, not from pretending problems do not exist. Financial confidence works the same way.

When you know the score, pressure decreases. Uncertainty shrinks. Decisions get easier.

Coach's Perspective

A coach would never let you guess your performance.

The film does not lie.

Know the score.

Details matter.

If you do not look at it, you cannot fix it.

Avoiding the box score does not change it. Reviewing it gives you control.

Coaches trust players who face reality. Financially, trusting yourself starts the same way.

Game Situations and Decision Points

You feel like you are doing fine, but your account balance never grows.

Do you blame income, or review spending?

You get a raise.

Do you upgrade your lifestyle immediately, or improve cash flow first?

You have debt but no clear picture of what you owe.

Do you ignore it, or list it out and face it?

Just like basketball, progress starts with honest evaluation.

Every adjustment begins with knowing where you stand.

Common Athlete Mistakes and Financial Parallels

Athletes rely on feel instead of film.

Financially, that means guessing instead of tracking.

Athletes avoid bad tape.

Financially, that means avoiding statements.

Athletes overvalue one good game.

Financially, that means one big paycheck hiding poor habits.

Short-term success can mask long-term problems. The box score exposes both.

Why This Step Changes Everything

Knowing your numbers changes your relationship with money.

It turns fear into information.

It turns stress into clarity.

It turns reaction into strategy.

You stop guessing. You stop hoping. You start adjusting.

This is how you stop playing from behind.

Winning the Long Game

Great teams know the score at all times, not just at the end of the game.

They know it in the first quarter.

They know it at halftime.

They know it before things get out of hand.

Knowing your financial snapshot is not about judgment. It is about awareness.

Awareness leads to control.

Control leads to confidence.

Confidence leads to better decisions.

This is how you move from survival mode to intentional progress.

Athlete Takeaways

Know the box score before you change the game plan.

Income means nothing without positive cash flow.

Assets build strength. Liabilities create pressure.

Fixed expenses create structure. Variable expenses create flexibility.

Watch the film. Awareness sets you up to win.

This is not about being perfect.

It is about knowing the score and playing the next possession better.

Chapter 3: Running the Offense: Budgeting and Saving

No team walks onto the court without an offensive plan.

You may adjust sets. You may read the defense. You may call different actions based on personnel or game flow. But there is always structure. Spacing matters. Roles matter. Shot selection matters. When teams abandon the offense and start freelancing, turnovers follow. Forced shots appear. Possessions get wasted. Momentum swings the wrong way.

Money works the same way.

Most people do not fail financially because they do not earn enough. They fail because they do not have a system. Spending happens reactively. Saving becomes optional. Decisions get made in the moment instead of within a plan. That is not running an offense. That is playing pickup and hoping talent carries you.

Talent alone does not win games. Structure does.

Budgeting and saving are how you install structure in your financial life.

Budgeting Systems That Actually Work

A budget is not punishment.

It is not restriction.

It is not saying no to everything.

It is not tracking every dollar obsessively.

A budget is an offensive system.

In basketball terms, budgeting is knowing where the ball is supposed to go. It creates spacing. It assigns roles. It keeps you from forcing shots late in the clock. You are not guessing possession by possession. You know what you are trying to run.

When players understand the offense, decision-making speeds up. When they do not, hesitation and mistakes follow. Money behaves the same way.

Good budgeting systems share a few traits.

They are simple.

They are realistic.

They are repeatable.

If a system is too complicated, you will not run it consistently. Coaches do not install plays players cannot execute under pressure. Your budget should work the same way.

At its core, budgeting answers three questions:

How much comes in?

What has to go out?

What is left to deploy intentionally?

That is the offense.

Everything else is detail.

Many people get stuck trying to create the perfect budget. Categories become too specific. Rules become too rigid. The system becomes fragile. Then one unexpected expense breaks it and people quit entirely.

A good offensive system can survive a broken play. A good budget can survive an imperfect month.

Why Athletes Resist Budgeting

Athletes resist budgeting for the same reason they resist rigid systems early in their careers.

It feels restrictive.

It feels boring.

It feels like someone else controlling decisions.

But veterans understand something younger players miss. Structure creates freedom.

When you know where the ball is supposed to go, you can play faster. When you know what money is supposed to do, decisions get easier. You stop negotiating with yourself every time something comes up.

Budgeting is not about limiting your life. It is about preventing chaos from making decisions for you.

Automating Savings Like Daily Shooting Reps

Nobody debates whether to take shooting reps.

You do them because they are built into the schedule. You do not wait to see if you feel like it. You do not decide based on mood. You show up and put in the work.

Saving should work the same way.

If you wait to save what is left over, you will rarely save anything. Life fills the space. Convenience wins. Discipline fades. There is always something else to spend on.

Automation fixes that.

Direct deposit.

Automatic transfers.

Scheduled contributions.

In basketball terms, this is daily shooting work. You may not see results immediately, but the reps compound. Form improves. Confidence builds. Consistency develops.

Automation removes emotion, and emotion is where financial mistakes live.

You are not relying on motivation. You are building a habit.

The most successful savers are not more disciplined. They simply removed the decision.

Why Saving First Changes Everything

Saving first flips the script.

Instead of asking, "Can I afford this?" after spending, you protect progress before life has a chance to interfere. You treat saving like a non-negotiable practice, not an optional extra.

This does two things.

First, it builds momentum.

Second, it reduces stress.

When savings grow automatically, pressure decreases. You stop feeling behind. You stop feeling one expense away from panic. Confidence follows preparation.

Emergency Funds as Injury Protection

Every athlete understands injury risk.

You do not plan to get hurt. You prepare anyway. Trainers exist. Rehab plans exist. Depth charts exist. Recovery protocols exist. Contact is part of the game.

An emergency fund is the financial version of that preparation.

It is cash set aside for the unexpected.

Car repairs.

Medical bills.

Job changes.

Delayed income.

Family emergencies.

Without an emergency fund, every surprise becomes a crisis. You reach for credit. You panic. You abandon the plan.

With an emergency fund, you stay composed. You handle the situation and keep running the offense.

That is staying in the game.

Emergency funds are not about pessimism. They are about realism. Games get physical. Life does too.

Why Athletes Skip Emergency Funds

Athletes often skip emergency funds because nothing has gone wrong yet.

That is dangerous thinking.

No coach waits for the first injury to prepare. You prepare because you know it will happen eventually, even if you do not know when.

Emergency funds buy time. Time prevents bad decisions. Bad decisions compound faster than good ones.

Balancing Lifestyle With Long-Term Goals

This is where many former athletes struggle the most.

You worked hard.

You sacrificed.

You trained when others rested.

You feel like you deserve to enjoy life.

That feeling is valid.

The mistake is turning short-term rewards into long-term damage.

Basketball teaches delayed gratification. You train when no one is watching so you can perform when it matters. Money requires the same discipline.

You do not have to live like a monk. You do have to be intentional.

Spend on what matters.

Cut what does not.

Protect future options.

Lifestyle should support your life, not quietly limit it.

Many financial problems come from lifestyle decisions that felt harmless at the time. Small upgrades compound. Fixed costs increase. Flexibility disappears.

That is how pressure builds without warning.

Why Lifestyle Creep Is So Dangerous

Lifestyle creep does not feel like failure.

It feels like progress.

Better apartment.

Better car.

More convenience.

More subscriptions.

None of it feels irresponsible in isolation. Over time, it locks in obligations that reduce options.

In basketball terms, this is adding minutes without improving recovery. Eventually, performance drops.

Strong players manage energy. Strong financial plans manage lifestyle.

Coach's Perspective

A coach would not overcomplicate this.

Do your job.

Be consistent.

Trust the system.

Do not cheat the work.

Budgets and savings are boring for the same reason shooting drills are boring. They work.

You do not win games by skipping fundamentals. You do not win financially by avoiding structure.

Game Situations and Decision Points

You get paid.

Do you save first or hope there is something left?

You want to upgrade your lifestyle.

Do you check the plan or ignore it?

An unexpected expense hits.

Do you stay calm or reach for credit?

These are possession-by-possession decisions. Over time, they decide outcomes.

No single choice ruins a season. Repeated choices define it.

Common Athlete Mistakes and Financial Parallels

Athletes skip fundamentals.

Financially, that looks like skipping savings.

Athletes overestimate what they can handle.

Financially, that leads to no emergency fund.

Athletes reward effort with shortcuts.

Financially, that shows up as lifestyle creep.

The same mistakes that lose games lose money.

Winning the Long Game

Running a clean offense is not about creativity. It is about execution.

Budgeting and saving give you control. Control creates freedom. Freedom allows you to make decisions from strength, not stress.

You do not need to be perfect. You need to be consistent.

This is how you stay composed when pressure shows up.

Athlete Takeaways

A budget is an offensive system, not a restriction.

Save first and make it automatic. Reps matter.

Emergency funds keep you calm under pressure.

Lifestyle choices today affect options tomorrow.

Execute the plan and trust the process.

You would never walk onto the court without knowing the offense.

Do not do it with your money.

Chapter 4: Credit, Debt, and Playing With Borrowed Minutes

Every basketball player understands the danger of foul trouble. You may be playing well. You may feel confident. You may even be controlling the game. But once you start picking up fouls, everything changes. Minutes become limited. Aggression turns into hesitation. You stop playing instinctively and start playing cautiously. One reach. One late rotation. One unnecessary foul. Suddenly you are on the bench watching the game instead of influencing it.

Debt works the same way.

Borrowed money gives you leverage, but it also puts conditions on how you play. It can help you move forward, or it can quietly limit your options. When debt is handled poorly, it rarely shows up immediately. It shows up later, when you need flexibility and realize you have none.

That is why credit and debt need to be understood, not feared.

Why Debt Feels Invisible at First

Foul trouble rarely feels urgent on the first whistle.

The first foul barely registers. The second one might feel unlucky. By the third, the coach is watching closely. By the fourth, everything tightens up. The problem was not the fourth foul. It was the pattern before it.

Debt behaves the same way.

A small balance feels manageable. A payment fits the budget. Another purchase seems harmless. Over time, obligations stack. Interest compounds. Flexibility disappears. By the time it feels serious, the options are already limited.

Debt does not announce itself as a problem. It becomes one quietly.

How Credit Scores and Reports Really Work

Your credit score is not a judgment of your character.

It is a record of how you handle borrowed minutes.

It looks at a few simple things:

Do you pay on time?

How much of your available credit do you use?

How long have you been using credit?

How often do you apply for new credit?

That is it.

In basketball terms, credit is trust. Coaches trust players who play under control. Officials trust players who defend without fouling. When you consistently execute, trust increases. When you reach, gamble, or foul unnecessarily, trust disappears quickly.

Your credit report is the film.

Your score is the grade.

You cannot argue with it. You cannot explain it away. You can only improve it through consistent behavior.

And just like film, it shows patterns, not isolated moments.

Why Credit Is Neutral Until You Use It

Credit itself is not good or bad.

It is neutral.

What matters is how you use it.

Credit cards, loans, and lines of credit are tools. Used correctly, they smooth cash flow and provide flexibility. Used poorly, they become expensive habits that drain momentum.

Interest is the cost of borrowing. It is the opposing team scoring points every possession you carry a balance.

One or two possessions might not hurt. Over time, it changes the entire game.

Credit Cards, Loans, and Interest

Credit cards are the most common source of trouble for athletes.

They are easy. They are convenient. They do not feel like debt when you swipe them. Payments seem manageable. Balances grow quietly.

Interest is what turns convenience into pressure.

The longer you carry a balance, the more interest compounds against you. That is like playing uphill basketball. You can still compete, but every mistake costs more.

Loans work the same way, just slower.

Car loans. Personal loans. Student loans. Mortgages. Each one carries an obligation that reduces flexibility.

Borrowed money should be used with intention, not convenience.

Why Minimum Payments Are Deceptive

Minimum payments feel safe.

They keep accounts current. They avoid penalties. They reduce stress in the moment. But they also stretch debt over long periods and maximize interest paid.

In basketball terms, minimum payments are like playing not to foul out instead of playing to win. You survive, but you never regain control.

Paying more than the minimum shortens the game. It reduces pressure. It restores flexibility.

Good Debt vs Bad Debt

Not all debt is the same.

Good debt helps you build something over time.

Education that increases earning potential.

A reasonably priced home that fits your life.

Business investments with a plan and margin.

Bad debt finances consumption.

Status purchases.

Lifestyle upgrades that fade quickly.

Impulse decisions that create long-term payments.

In basketball terms, good debt is investing in development. Weight room. Skill work. Film study. Bad debt is chasing highlights at the expense of fundamentals.

The difference is not the interest rate alone. It is whether the debt creates future options or takes them away.

Why Athletes Struggle With This Distinction

Athletes are used to betting on themselves.

That confidence is earned. It wins games. Financially, it can create exposure.

Assuming future income will cover today's decisions is one of the fastest ways athletes lose control of debt. Careers change. Roles change. Injuries happen. Opportunities shift.

Debt does not adjust when circumstances do.

Debt Traps That Kill Momentum

Most debt problems come from simple traps.

Using credit to fund lifestyle.

Ignoring balances because payments feel manageable.

Co-signing without understanding the risk.

Assuming future income will fix today's decisions.

None of these feel reckless in the moment. They feel reasonable. That is what makes them dangerous.

Athletes often feel confident in their ability to recover. That confidence wins games. Financially, it can put you in foul trouble early.

Debt does not care how hard you work.

It only cares how consistently you pay.

Once momentum is lost, it is hard to get it back.

The Hidden Risk of Co-Signing

Co-signing is one of the most misunderstood decisions athletes make.

You are not helping someone "just in case."

You are fully responsible if they do not pay.

In basketball terms, co-signing is committing a foul for someone else's mistake. You take the penalty. You lose the minutes.

Relationships do not change how credit reports work.

Why High Income Does Not Cancel Debt Risk

High income masks debt problems temporarily.

Payments feel affordable. Stress feels low. But income volatility exposes debt quickly. If income drops, obligations remain.

That is like playing extended minutes while injured. You can survive for a while. Eventually performance drops.

Debt should be manageable at your worst month, not just your best.

Coach's Perspective

A coach would be direct.

Value every possession.

Know the situation.

Do not beat yourself.

Play smart minutes.

Debt magnifies decisions. Handle it with respect.

Good teams foul less because they are disciplined, not passive. Good financial plans use debt carefully, not fearfully.

Game Situations and Decision Points

You can put it on a card.

Do you do it because it fits the plan or because it is easy?

You qualify for a loan.

Do you ask if you should take it or just if you can?

Someone asks you to co-sign.

Do you understand the consequences or feel pressured?

These are late-game decisions. Awareness matters.

Common Athlete Mistakes and Financial Parallels

Athletes chase comfort early.

Financially, that shows up as lifestyle debt.

Athletes trust momentum too much.

Financially, that leads to over-borrowing.

Athletes ignore small mistakes.

Financially, that becomes long-term damage.

Foul trouble is rarely one bad call. It is repeated poor decisions.

Winning the Long Game

Borrowed minutes can help or hurt you.

The difference is discipline.

Play within your system.

Protect flexibility.

Avoid unnecessary fouls.

The goal is not to avoid credit entirely. The goal is to use it without losing control.

Smart players stay on the floor because they understand the situation.

Athlete Takeaways

Credit is trust. Protect it.

Interest works against you if you are careless.

Borrow to build, not to impress.

Understand debt before it limits your minutes.

Smart decisions keep you on the floor.

Debt does not bench you immediately.

It benches you later.

The best players never let it get that far.

Chapter 5: The Locker Room of Money: Banking Basics

Every team has a locker room.

It is not glamorous. Fans do not see it. Highlights are never filmed there. But everything that happens on the court depends on it. That is where gear is stored, meetings happen, and preparation begins. It is where players get organized before the game and reset afterward.

When the locker room is disorganized, everything else suffers. Shoes are missing. Equipment is misplaced. Meetings start late. Focus drifts. Small issues turn into distractions that bleed into performance.

Your banking system is the locker room of your money.

Most people do not think about it until something goes wrong. Fees show up unexpectedly. Payments miss. Fraud appears. Accounts overdraft. Stress increases. When the locker room is messy, it becomes impossible to execute at a high level.

Before you worry about investing, growth, or building wealth, your locker room has to function.

Why Banking Problems Create More Stress Than They Should

Banking problems rarely feel urgent at first.

A small fee here. A late transfer there. An overdraft that feels like a one-time mistake. But when systems are loose, these issues repeat. Over time, they create frustration and mental clutter.

In basketball terms, this is like constantly worrying about your shoes slipping or your jersey being wrong. You can still play, but you are distracted. You are not fully focused on execution.

A clean banking system removes friction. It lets you focus on bigger decisions without worrying about the basics.

Checking vs Savings Accounts

Checking accounts are for movement.

Savings accounts are for storage.

Checking is where money flows in and out. Paychecks. Bills. Day-to-day spending. Automatic payments. It is active and constantly moving.

Savings is where money sits with purpose. Emergency funds. Short-term goals. Protection. It is not meant to be touched casually.

In basketball terms, checking is the court. Savings is the bench.

You need both.

If everything is on the court all the time, you are exposed. One bad possession, one unexpected hit, and you have no protection. If everything is on the bench, nothing is happening. The game never starts.

Blurring the two creates confusion and bad habits. When savings is too accessible, it gets spent. When checking is overloaded, stress increases.

Separation creates clarity.

Why Separation Changes Behavior

Most people do not overspend because they lack discipline. They overspend because money is too easy to access.

When savings and checking are blended, every dollar feels available. There is no mental barrier. That makes impulse decisions easier and protection weaker.

Separating accounts creates friction in a good way. It forces a pause. That pause is often enough to prevent mistakes.

In basketball terms, this is spacing. Proper spacing makes good decisions easier. Poor spacing leads to forced shots and turnovers.

Online Banks vs Traditional Banks

Traditional banks offer branches, tellers, and face-to-face service. Online banks often offer lower fees, better interest rates, and convenience.

There is no universal right answer.

The right choice is the one that fits your system.

Some athletes prefer in-person access. They like being able to walk into a branch and talk to someone. Others value efficiency, automation, and lower costs.

What matters is not which type you choose. What matters is understanding:

What fees you are paying

How accessible your money is

How fast transfers happen

What protections are in place

In basketball terms, this is scheme fit. You do not run someone else's offense just because it works for them. You run what fits your personnel and strengths.

Why Convenience Can Be Dangerous

Convenience is powerful.

Auto-pay. One-click transfers. Instant access. These tools save time, but they also hide mistakes if you are not paying attention.

When everything runs automatically and you never check, small problems grow unnoticed. Fraud goes undetected longer. Fees stack quietly. Balances drift lower than expected.

Automation should reduce work, not eliminate awareness.

How Money Actually Moves Electronically

Money does not move magically.

It flows through systems.

Direct deposit

Electronic transfers

Debit cards

Automatic bill pay

Pending transactions

Processing delays

Timing matters.

Knowing when money leaves and when it arrives is critical. Missed transfers cause overdrafts. Delayed deposits create stress. Pending charges make balances look higher than they actually are.

In basketball terms, this is clock awareness. You do not take a shot without knowing the time. Banking works the same way. Awareness prevents unnecessary fouls.

Why Overdrafts Are Usually System Failures

Overdrafts feel like mistakes. Most of the time, they are system failures.

Bills hitting before deposits clear

Balances not accounting for pending charges

Savings being too accessible

Alerts not set

Fixing the system prevents the mistake from happening again.

Blaming yourself without fixing structure leads to repeat problems.

Protecting Yourself From Fraud and Overdrafts

Fraud and overdrafts thrive in loose systems.

You protect yourself by:

Monitoring accounts regularly

Setting alerts for transactions and low balances

Keeping a buffer in checking

Separating savings from spending

Reviewing statements consistently

In basketball terms, this is defensive positioning. Sloppy defense gets exposed. Clean defense forces the other team to make tough decisions.

Most banking problems are not dramatic. They are preventable.

Why Alerts Are Like Communication on Defense

Alerts are not paranoia. They are communication.

A notification for a large transaction

A warning for low balance

A notice for unusual activity

These are teammates talking on defense. Silence leads to breakdowns. Communication keeps everyone aligned.

Coach's Perspective

A coach would keep it simple.

Protect the locker room.

Details matter.

Handle your business.

Do not create your own problems.

Coaches hate distractions. Banking chaos is a distraction you can eliminate.

Banking is not exciting. It is foundational.

Game Situations and Decision Points

You have one account for everything.

Do you separate systems or keep guessing?

You get hit with a fee.

Do you fix the structure or ignore it?

You notice a suspicious charge.

Do you act immediately or hope it resolves itself?

These are small moments. Over time, they decide outcomes.

Common Athlete Mistakes and Financial Parallels

Athletes ignore details.

Financially, that shows up as fees and errors.

Athletes trust systems blindly.

Financially, that leads to missed fraud.

Athletes avoid boring work.

Financially, that leads to chaos.

The fundamentals matter even when they are boring.

Why Clean Systems Create Confidence

When your banking is clean, stress drops.

Bills are paid on time.

Balances make sense.

Savings grows quietly.

Unexpected issues are manageable.

Confidence comes from control. Control comes from systems.

That confidence shows up everywhere else in your financial life.

Winning the Long Game

A clean locker room supports everything else.

Good banking does not make headlines. It does not create highlights. But it keeps you organized, protected, and ready to execute when opportunities show up.

You cannot build wealth on a messy foundation.

Athlete Takeaways

Checking is for movement. Savings is for protection.

Choose banks that fit your system, not someone else's.

Know how and when your money moves.

Protect against fraud the same way you protect the ball.

Clean systems keep you in control.

You would never accept a disorganized locker room on game day.

Do not accept one with your money either.

Part II: Defense, Protection, and Staying in the Game

D*efense keeps you on the floor when shots are not falling.*

Every basketball player knows this truth.

You will not always shoot well. There will be cold nights, bad matchups, and stretches where nothing seems to drop. What determines whether you stay in the game during those moments is not your scoring. It is your defense.

Defense is effort. Awareness. Positioning. Communication. It is doing the work that rarely shows up in the highlights but keeps you trusted by coaches. Players who defend stay on the floor. Players who do not, sit.

Money works the same way.

You can earn well. You can make smart decisions. You can have momentum. None of it matters if one bad event knocks you out of the game. An injury. A lawsuit. A missed payment. A lack of protection. Financial defense is not exciting, but it is essential.

This section of the playbook is about staying available.

Defense in your financial life is not about fear or playing small. It is about awareness and preparation. It is understanding what could hurt you and putting systems in place before those risks show up. Just like basketball, you cannot eliminate risk. You can manage it.

Athletes often focus on offense first. That makes sense. Basketball rewards scoring. Life rewards income. But championship teams understand balance. They score and they defend. They take care of the ball. They protect leads.

They avoid unnecessary fouls.

Financial defense includes understanding risk, using insurance correctly, and protecting what you have already worked to build. It is knowing when to push and when to slow the game. It is staying disciplined when everything feels under control so you are not exposed when it is not.

Skipping defense is betting everything on perfection.

Perfection does not exist.

The players who last are the ones who can contribute even when shots are not falling. The same is true financially. Protection keeps you in the game long enough for offense to matter.

This section will show you how to build that defense.

How to stay composed when life gets physical.

How to protect your future possessions.

How to avoid fouls that limit your minutes.

Because winning is not just about scoring.

It is about staying on the floor.

Chapter 6: Risk Awareness and Decision Making

Every basketball player recognizes this moment.

The game is tight. The crowd is loud. Momentum is swinging. Someone on the bench calls for a big play. Maybe a quick three in transition. Maybe a hard drive into traffic. Something aggressive to change the energy.

Great players pause.

Not because they are afraid, but because they understand the situation. The score. The clock. The matchup. Who is in foul trouble. Who is tired. Who has the hot hand. Risk is never just about the shot itself. It is about everything surrounding it.

Money decisions work the same way.

Risk is not about what sounds exciting, what worked for someone else, or what looks impressive on the surface. It is about what fits your real situation. Understanding risk is what keeps you from forcing plays that feel bold in the moment but cost you later.

Why Athletes Struggle With Risk Outside the Game

Athletes are trained to take risks.

You are rewarded for confidence. You are taught to attack, not hesitate. You learn that playing scared leads to mistakes. Over time, that mindset becomes part of your identity.

That mindset wins games.

It can also create problems with money.

Financial risk does not behave like competitive risk. You cannot always make up for a mistake with extra effort. There is no overtime for poor financial decisions. Some outcomes are permanent.

Understanding that difference is the first step toward smarter decision-making.

Emotional Risk vs Financial Risk

Emotional risk is how you feel about uncertainty.

Financial risk is how much damage you can actually absorb.

Athletes often confuse the two.

Emotionally, you may feel comfortable taking risks. You have competed under pressure your entire life. You trust your ability to recover from mistakes. You believe you will figure it out if something goes wrong.

Financially, that may not be true.

If one bad outcome would force you into debt, derail your career, strain relationships, or push you to sell investments at the worst possible time, your financial risk capacity is lower than your confidence suggests.

In basketball terms, this is knowing the difference between wanting the ball and being the right option in that moment.

Sometimes the best player takes the shot. Sometimes the smartest play is to move the ball and trust the system.

Risk Capacity Changes Over Time

Risk is not fixed.

Your ability to take risk changes as your life changes.

Early in a career, you may have fewer responsibilities but less income. Later, you may have more income but more people depending on you. Injuries, career transitions, family changes, and unexpected events all affect how much risk you can handle.

In basketball terms, this is understanding your role on the team.

A young player with depth behind them can play aggressively. A veteran carrying minutes cannot afford careless fouls. The same logic applies to money.

Ignoring changes in risk capacity leads to forced decisions later.

Time Horizon and Flexibility

Time horizon matters more than most people realize.

If you need money soon, you cannot afford large swings. Volatility becomes dangerous when there is no time to recover. If money is meant for decades from now, short-term ups and downs matter less.

Flexibility is the hidden variable.

Do you have savings?

Do you have stable income?

Can you adjust spending if something goes wrong?

Do you have support systems?

A deep team can take more chances. A team dealing with injuries cannot. Money works the same way.

Time and flexibility determine how much risk you can realistically take, not how confident you feel.

Why Volatility Feels Worse Than It Is

Many athletes mistake volatility for failure.

Seeing balances drop triggers the same emotional response as missing shots or losing games. The instinct is to react. Change strategy. Force something to happen.

But volatility is not the enemy. It is movement.

Permanent loss is the enemy.

In basketball terms, volatility is giving up a run. Permanent loss is losing the game because you abandoned fundamentals.

Understanding the difference helps you stay composed when numbers move.

How Risk Affects Every Money Decision

Risk is not limited to investing.

It affects:

How much cash you keep

How much debt you take on

What insurance coverage you need

How aggressive your lifestyle choices are

How concentrated your income is

Ignoring risk does not make you bold. It makes you exposed.

Every decision should be filtered through one simple question:

What happens if this does not go my way?

If the answer creates panic, the risk may be too high. Awareness is the difference between smart aggression and reckless play.

Knowing When to Push and When to Slow the Game

Great basketball players understand tempo.

Sometimes the right move is to push. Attack before the defense sets. Take advantage of momentum. Apply pressure.

Other times, the smartest play is to slow it down. Run the offense. Protect the ball. Get good shots. Manage the clock.

Money requires the same awareness.

There are moments to invest aggressively.

There are moments to protect cash.

There are times to take on risk.

There are times to prioritize stability.

The mistake is playing one speed all the time.

Aggressive all the time leads to mistakes.

Conservative all the time leads to stagnation.

Winning decisions are situational, not emotional.

Why Copying Other People's Risk Fails

One of the most common mistakes athletes make is copying someone else's strategy.

A teammate invests aggressively.

A former player talks about real estate wins.

Someone on social media posts big returns.

What you do not see is their full situation. Their income stability. Their safety net. Their time horizon. Their mistakes.

Running someone else's offense without understanding it leads to turnovers. Money is no different.

Your plan has to fit your life.

Coach's Perspective

A coach would say it plainly.

Know the situation.

Do not put the team in a bad spot.

Control what you can control.

Play smart.

Coaches do not eliminate risk. They manage it.

Risk is part of the game. Poor awareness is optional.

Game Situations and Decision Points

You hear about an aggressive opportunity.

Do you ask if it fits your timeline or just if it has upside?

You consider a big purchase.

Do you evaluate flexibility if income changes?

You feel confident and want to take more risk.

Do you check the downside first?

These moments look small. Over time, they decide outcomes.

Common Athlete Mistakes and Financial Parallels

Athletes trust confidence over context.

Financially, that leads to overexposure.

Athletes chase momentum.

Financially, that leads to poor timing.

Athletes ignore fatigue and limits.

Financially, that leads to stress and forced decisions.

The same mistakes that lose games lose money.

Winning the Long Game

Risk cannot be eliminated.

Loss can be managed.

The athletes who succeed long-term understand their limits and respect them. They take risks when it makes sense and protect themselves when it does not.

That is not fear.

That is discipline.

Championship players are not reckless. They are aware. They know when to attack and when to trust the system.

Money rewards the same mindset.

Athlete Takeaways

Confidence does not equal capacity. Know the difference.

Time horizon shapes every risk decision.

Flexibility gives you options under pressure.

Push when it fits. Slow down when it does not.

Smart risk keeps you in the game.

The goal is not to avoid risk.

The goal is to take the right risks at the right time and stay on the floor long enough to win.

Chapter 7: Insurance Fundamentals Every Player Needs

Staying on the Floor: Insurance as Financial Defense

Every basketball player learns this lesson sooner or later.

You can do everything right and still get hurt.

You can lift, condition, stretch, eat right, watch film, follow the scouting report, and still land on someone's foot. One awkward step, one unexpected collision, one split second where timing is off, and the game changes. Not because you lacked effort or discipline, but because basketball is a contact sport. Bodies collide. Momentum shifts. Chaos shows up without warning.

That reality is why teams do not just hope for the best.

They invest heavily in trainers, medical staff, strength coaches, physical therapists, and deep benches. They build redundancy into the roster. They assume injuries will happen at some point and prepare accordingly. Not because they expect failure, but because availability matters.

Insurance serves the same role in your financial life.

You do not buy insurance because you expect something bad to happen. You buy it because contact is part of life. Accidents happen. Illness happens. Lawsuits happen. Weather happens. Insurance is not about fear or pessimism. It is about staying available when the unexpected shows up.

In basketball terms, insurance is defense. It does not score points. It does not show up on the highlight reel. But without it, one hit can end the season.

Health Insurance Is Not Optional

Health insurance is non-negotiable.

It covers doctor visits, prescriptions, preventative care, emergency treatment, surgeries, and catastrophic medical events that can destroy your finances in a single afternoon. Without coverage, one injury or illness can wipe out years of progress, derail your career plans, and force decisions you never wanted to make.

Many athletes fall into the same trap early in adulthood.

They assume youth equals safety.

They feel strong. They recover quickly. They have not been seriously hurt before. So they treat health insurance like a luxury instead of a requirement. That mindset works until it does not.

Skipping health insurance is the financial equivalent of playing without ankle support. You might feel faster. You might save money. You might even be fine for a while. But when contact happens, the damage is real and there is no rewind button.

Having health insurance is only step one. Understanding it is step two.

You need to know what plan you have.

You need to know what it covers.

You need to know what it does not cover.

That means understanding deductibles, copays, coinsurance, networks, and out-of-pocket maximums. It means knowing whether your doctor is in-network, what happens in an emergency, and how prescriptions are handled. These details matter because confusion leads to mistakes, and mistakes get expensive fast.

A coach would never say, "Just go out there and play. Do not worry about the scheme."

Knowing your coverage is knowing the game plan.

Auto and Renters Insurance: Protecting Everyday Risk

Auto insurance and renters insurance are two of the most overlooked forms of protection, especially among young athletes and early-career professionals.

Auto insurance protects you, your vehicle, your passengers, and anyone else involved in an accident. It also protects your future income and assets if you are found responsible for damage or injury.

Renters insurance protects your personal property and provides liability coverage if someone gets hurt where you live or if damage you cause affects others.

These are not optional background expenses. They are foundational.

Athletes tend to focus on visible costs like rent, car payments, training expenses, and travel. Insurance fades into the background because it feels abstract. Accidents do not feel real until they happen.

But accidents do not announce themselves.

One distracted driver.

One icy road.

One spilled drink that damages a neighbor's unit.

One guest who slips and gets hurt.

The financial consequences of those moments can dwarf the cost of years of premiums.

In basketball terms, auto and renters insurance protect your positioning. One bad possession should not turn into a ten-point swing. Insurance absorbs the shock so you can keep playing instead of scrambling to recover.

Homeowners Insurance: Protecting the Big Asset

If and when you own a home, homeowners insurance becomes essential.

It protects the structure of the home, your personal belongings, and your liability exposure. It also covers risks most people never think about until they are living through them. Fires. Storms. Water damage. Theft. Lawsuits. Injuries on your property.

Owning property without proper insurance is like playing defense with no help behind you. Everything looks fine until one breakdown leads to an easy score. And once that happens, you are chasing the game.

As your life grows, your coverage needs to grow too.

More assets mean more exposure. Higher income means more liability. More responsibility means less room for mistakes. Insurance is not static. It should evolve as your situation changes.

Protection that made sense when you were renting a small apartment may be wildly inadequate once you own a home, have dependents, or build significant net worth.

Defense must scale with the opponent.

Premiums, Deductibles, and Coverage Limits

This is where many people get confused, frustrated, or disengaged.

Premiums are what you pay to keep coverage active.

Deductibles are what you pay out of pocket before insurance starts paying.

Coverage limits are the maximum amount the policy will pay.

There is always a trade-off.

Higher deductibles usually mean lower premiums.

Lower deductibles usually mean higher premiums.

There is no free lunch. Anyone who promises full protection with no cost is selling fiction.

The goal is balance.

You want coverage you can afford to maintain consistently. You want deductibles you can handle without panic. Insurance is not about getting every dollar back. It is about preventing financial catastrophe.

In basketball terms, you are not trying to block every shot. You are trying to prevent easy baskets and momentum swings. Smart defense forces tough shots and keeps the game manageable.

A Coach's Perspective

A coach would not overthink this.

Protect yourself.

Know your assignments.

Stay available.

Do not leave yourself exposed.

Insurance is not about being cautious or timid. It is about being responsible to yourself, your teammates, and your future. You cannot help the team if you are sidelined. You cannot build wealth if one incident wipes you out financially.

The best players stay on the floor.

Game Situations and Decision Points

Every athlete faces these moments.

You feel healthy and consider skipping coverage. Do you save a little money now, or do you protect against an unknown that could cost everything later?

You choose the cheapest policy available. Do you actually understand what it covers and what it excludes?

You assume nothing bad will happen. Are you prepared if it does?

These are not emotional decisions. They are professional ones. Professionals manage risk. They do not ignore it.

Common Athlete Mistakes and Financial Parallels

Athletes underestimate injury risk.

Financially, this shows up as skipping coverage or delaying protection.

Athletes focus on cost instead of impact.

Financially, this leads to underinsuring and false savings.

Athletes ignore details.

Financially, this results in unpleasant surprises when coverage is needed most.

The same habits that hurt athletes on the court hurt them with money. The same discipline that creates longevity in sports creates stability in finances.

Winning the Long Game

Insurance does not win games.

It keeps you in them.

You cannot control injuries, accidents, lawsuits, or unexpected events. You can control how prepared you are when they happen. Protection allows you to absorb hits, stay upright, and keep moving forward.

That is defense.

That is professionalism.

That is how careers and financial lives last.

Athlete Takeaways

Health insurance is mandatory, not optional.

Auto and renters insurance protect against everyday risk.

Homeowners insurance protects assets and liability.

Premiums, deductibles, and limits are trade-offs. Know yours.

Staying insured keeps you on the floor.

Defense does not get the glory. But without it, the season ends early.

Chapter 8: Life, Disability, and Liability Coverage

The Financial Depth Chart: Staying Available When Life Hits Back

Every coach plans for injuries, even if they never say it out loud. Depth charts exist because availability is never guaranteed. Coaches know that bodies break down. They know that a rolled ankle, a torn ligament, or a freak collision can change rotations instantly. Teams do not assume disaster is coming, but they absolutely prepare for it. When a starter goes down, the season does not have to end because systems, backups, and contingencies are already in place.

Life works the same way.

In your financial life, life insurance, disability insurance, and liability coverage function as your depth chart. They are not glamorous. They do not get headlines. You never hear anyone brag about them. But when something unexpected happens, they determine whether you stay in the game or are forced to the sideline.

Preparation is not pessimism. It is professionalism.

Life Insurance Is About People, Not Products

Life insurance exists for one reason. To protect people who depend on you.

If your absence would create financial hardship for someone else, life insurance matters. If no one relies on your income yet, it may not be necessary right now. The purpose is protection, not complexity and not investment performance.

Many athletes misunderstand life insurance because they are introduced to it the wrong way. They hear sales pitches before they understand the purpose. That creates confusion and resistance.

At its core, life insurance is simple.

If someone needs your income to survive or maintain stability, you insure against the risk of that income disappearing. That could include a spouse, children, parents, or even business partners depending on the situation.

Life insurance is not about you. It is about everyone else.

Term Life Insurance: The Starting Five

Term life insurance covers you for a specific period of time. Ten years. Twenty years. Thirty years. It is designed to protect income during key stages of life when financial obligations are highest.

Starting a career.

Raising a family.

Paying off a mortgage.

Building stability.

Term insurance is straightforward. You pay a premium. If you pass away during the term, the policy pays a death benefit to your beneficiaries. If you outlive the term, the coverage ends.

It is affordable.

It is efficient.

It does its job.

For most former student-athletes early in their financial lives, term insurance is the right first move. It covers the risk without draining cash flow or adding unnecessary complexity.

In basketball terms, term insurance is your reliable starter. It plays heavy minutes, does the fundamentals well, and fits the system. You do not need trick plays when the basics are not yet mastered.

Permanent Life Insurance: Specialty Sets, Not Opening Tip

Permanent life insurance lasts your entire life and includes additional features beyond a death benefit. It costs more. It requires careful planning. It is not automatically good or bad, but it is often misunderstood.

Permanent coverage can make sense in certain situations.

Long-term estate planning.

Special needs planning.

Advanced tax strategies.

Business succession planning.

But for many young professionals and former athletes, permanent insurance is not the right first step. Installing specialty sets before the fundamentals are solid creates confusion and unnecessary strain.

You do not open a game running exotic plays if you cannot execute a basic offense. You build from the ground up.

Disability Insurance: Protecting the Engine

This is one of the most overlooked forms of protection for athletes and non-athletes alike.

People insure their car.

They insure their phone.

They insure their apartment.

They insure their furniture.

Yet many fail to insure the one thing that produces everything else. Their ability to earn income.

Disability insurance replaces a portion of your income if injury or illness prevents you from working. It does not just protect against catastrophic events. It protects cash flow during recovery periods that can last months or years.

If income stops, everything else stops with it.

Rent.

Food.

Debt payments.

Savings.

Insurance premiums.

In basketball terms, this is protecting availability. If you cannot play, the offense stalls. If you cannot work, the financial plan collapses.

Athletes are conditioned to grind through pain. That mentality builds toughness and resilience on the court. Financially, it can be dangerous. Some injuries do not allow for grinding. Some illnesses do not care how hard you work.

Disability insurance exists to bridge that gap.

Short-Term vs Long-Term Disability

Short-term disability typically covers a few months of income replacement.

Long-term disability can cover years or even decades depending on the policy.

Employer plans often provide some coverage, but they are rarely enough on their own. They may cap benefits. They may be taxable. They may not follow you if you change jobs.

Knowing what coverage you have and what gaps exist is critical. Just like understanding your role on the team, clarity prevents surprises.

Umbrella Liability Coverage: The Last Line of Defense

Umbrella insurance provides additional liability protection on top of auto and homeowners insurance.

As income and assets grow, exposure grows. The more you earn and own, the more attractive you become as a legal target. One accident, one misunderstanding, or one bad moment can turn into a lawsuit that exceeds basic coverage limits.

Umbrella coverage exists for rare but devastating scenarios.

Serious auto accidents.

Major injuries on your property.

Claims that escalate beyond expectations.

In basketball terms, this is help defense. You hope the system works and everyone stays in front of their assignment. But when something breaks down, help defense prevents the easy score.

Umbrella policies are relatively inexpensive for the amount of protection they provide. They are not about paranoia. They are about recognizing reality.

Common Insurance Mistakes Athletes Make

The same mistakes show up again and again.

Assuming youth equals safety.

Skipping coverage because nothing has happened yet.

Buying the cheapest policy without understanding what it covers.

Insuring possessions but not income.

Failing to update coverage as life changes.

Insurance mistakes are silent. They do not hurt right away. They wait until the stakes are highest. That is when the consequences show up.

Just like conditioning, you do not feel the benefits until you need them.

A Coach's Perspective

A coach would not sugarcoat this.

Protect the team.

Protect availability.

Do not let one hit end the season.

Prepare for what you cannot control.

Coverage is not fear. It is responsibility. It is respect for the work you have already put in and the people who depend on you.

No coach benches preparation.

Game Situations and Decision Points

These moments define professionals.

You feel healthy and invincible. Do you rely on confidence or prepare for reality?

Your income increases. Do you update coverage or remain exposed?

You assume lawsuits happen to other people. Do you prepare anyway?

These are not emotional decisions. They are professional ones. Professionals manage risk even when things are going well.

Athlete Habits and Financial Parallels

Athletes ignore depth.

Financially, that means no backup plan.

Athletes underestimate risk.

Financially, that means inadequate coverage.

Athletes delay uncomfortable decisions.

Financially, that leads to exposure.

The same habits that shorten careers on the court shorten financial stability off it. Discipline translates everywhere.

Winning the Long Game

You cannot control injuries, illness, or legal risk.

You can control preparation.

Life insurance protects people.

Disability insurance protects income.

Liability coverage protects everything else.

Together, they form your financial depth chart.

That is how professionals stay available across long seasons and long lives.

Athlete Takeaways

Life insurance protects people, not paydays.

Term coverage is usually the right first move.

Disability insurance protects your ability to earn.

Umbrella coverage protects against worst-case scenarios.

Preparation keeps you in the game.

Availability is not luck. It is built.

Part III: Scoring With Purpose (Investing Fundamentals)

S*mart shots, good spacing, and patience win games.*

Every great offense has discipline.

The ball moves. Players know their spots. Shots come from rhythm, not desperation. When teams start forcing the action, efficiency drops and momentum disappears. Good offenses understand that scoring is not about taking the most shots. It is about taking the right ones.

Investing works the same way.

This is the part of the playbook most athletes are excited about. Growth. Momentum. Results. But just like basketball, the mistake is trying to score too fast. Heat checks replace shot selection. Movement replaces purpose. Emotion replaces execution.

Smart investing is not aggressive. It is intentional.

This section is about learning how to score without forcing the game. It focuses on understanding how financial markets actually work, what you own when you invest, and why patience matters more than activity. You will learn how different investments play different roles, how diversification creates spacing, and how time rewards discipline.

Just like basketball, offense only works when the fundamentals are solid. If you skipped the preseason or ignored defense, investing becomes reckless. If you build this part on a strong foundation, it becomes powerful.

Markets will have cold streaks. There will be stretches where progress feels slow. The temptation to change strategies, chase trends, or abandon the plan will show up. This is where discipline matters most.

Great players trust the system.

They move without the ball.

They wait for the right look.

They take high-quality shots even if the crowd wants more.

Great investors do the same.

This section will help you understand how to score over time, not just in one possession. How to let spacing and patience work in your favor. How to avoid turnovers caused by emotion and overconfidence.

Scoring with purpose is not about excitement.

It is about efficiency.

It is about consistency.

It is about letting the game come to you.

That is how wins are built.

Chapter 9: How the Financial Markets Really Work

When the Game Slows Down: Understanding Markets Without the Noise

Every basketball player remembers the first time the game felt fast. The ball moved quicker than expected. Passing lanes closed instantly. Defenders seemed to appear out of nowhere. What looked smooth and controlled on film felt chaotic on the floor. Decisions had to be made in fractions of a second, and hesitation got punished.

Then something changed.

It was not that the game slowed down. The speed stayed the same. What changed was your understanding. You learned spacing. You recognized tendencies. You anticipated rotations. What once felt frantic started to feel readable. You were no longer reacting. You were processing.

The financial markets work the same way.

To people outside the system, markets look random and overwhelming. Numbers move constantly. Headlines scream urgency. Opinions pour in from every direction. It feels like chaos. But underneath the noise is structure. Once you understand how markets actually function, the panic fades. The movements make sense. The speed becomes manageable.

The market does not slow down.

You get better at seeing the game.

What Markets Actually Do

At their core, financial markets exist for one primary purpose.

They connect people who need capital with people willing to provide it.

Companies raise money to grow. They build products, hire employees, expand operations, and invest in new ideas. Governments borrow money to fund infrastructure, education, defense, and public services. Investors provide that capital in exchange for ownership, interest, or future repayment.

That exchange is the engine of the market.

Prices move based on expectations about the future, not just what is happening today. Earnings forecasts. Economic conditions. Interest rates. Innovation. Risk. Confidence. Fear. All of it gets reflected in real time.

In basketball terms, the market is the league itself.

Teams compete.

Some rebuild.

Some dominate.

Others struggle.

Standings change.

Rules evolve.

But the season keeps moving forward.

Markets are not designed to feel comfortable. They are designed to function. Discomfort is part of the process, not a signal that something is broken.

Ownership Versus Lending: Stocks and Bonds

Two of the most important building blocks in investing are stocks and bonds.

Stocks represent ownership. When you buy a stock, you own a piece of a company. You participate in its growth. You benefit when it succeeds. You also share in the downside when it struggles.

Ownership comes with volatility. The upside is higher, but the path is uneven.

Bonds are loans. When you buy a bond, you lend money to a company or government. In return, you receive interest and expect repayment of principal. The upside is lower, but the structure is more predictable.

In basketball terms, stocks are your scorers.

They create offense.

They stretch the floor.

They drive growth.

They can swing games.

Bonds are your defenders.

They provide stability.

They control pace.

They reduce volatility.

They protect leads.

You do not win championships with offense alone. You need balance. A roster overloaded with scorers and no defense gets exposed. A portfolio built without balance behaves the same way.

Investing is not betting. It is owning and lending to productive assets over time. The goal is not to guess what happens next week. The goal is to participate in long-term growth while managing risk.

Market Cycles and the Reality of Volatility

Markets move in cycles.

Expansion.

Slowdown.

Contraction.

Recovery.

Repeat.

This pattern is not a flaw. It is a feature. Economic systems breathe. Growth stretches resources. Pullbacks reset expectations. Recoveries rebuild momentum.

Volatility is simply movement.

It is not failure.

It is not a mistake.

It is not a sign that the system is broken.

In basketball terms, volatility is momentum. No team dominates every quarter. Runs happen. Cold stretches happen. Adjustments get made. The scoreboard changes throughout the game.

Athletes who panic during volatility make the same mistake as players who abandon the offense after one bad possession. They confuse short-term discomfort with long-term failure.

The market's job is not to be smooth.

Its job is to reflect changing conditions.

The Trap of Heat Checks

Every basketball player understands the temptation of a heat check.

You hit two shots.

Then three.

The crowd reacts.

Confidence spikes.

The next shot feels automatic.

Sometimes it goes in.

Sometimes it does not.

In markets, heat checks show up as chasing what is working right now. The hottest stock. The newest trend. The investment everyone is talking about. It feels logical. It feels urgent. It feels smart in the moment.

Over time, it rarely is.

Long-term investing is about shot selection, not shot volume. It is about repeatedly taking high-quality opportunities that fit your role, your timeline, and your plan. It is not about forcing action because recent results look good.

In basketball terms, long-term strategy is running the offense.

Good spacing.

Ball movement.

Patience.

High-percentage looks.

Heat checks are contested shots early in the clock. They occasionally work. Over time, they wreck efficiency and momentum.

Trusting the System Over the Moment

Markets reward discipline far more consistently than they reward excitement.

This is where many athletes struggle. Sports train you to react quickly. To adjust instantly. To respond emotionally to momentum. That instinct is valuable on the court. Financially, it can be dangerous.

Great investors are not hyperactive.

They are consistent.

They trust systems.

They rebalance.

They stay invested.

They avoid emotional decisions driven by headlines or short-term noise.

In basketball terms, they do not abandon the offense because of a missed shot. They trust spacing, timing, and repetition.

A Coach's Perspective

A coach would say it plainly.

Trust the system.

Move the ball.

Take good shots.

Do not force the game.

Coaches understand that execution matters more than emotion. One bad quarter does not define a season. One losing streak does not mean the playbook is wrong.

Markets reward discipline, not impatience. The teams that survive adversity are the ones that do not panic when things feel uncomfortable.

Game Situations and Decision Points

These moments separate amateurs from professionals.

The market drops sharply. Do you panic and sell, or do you stay committed to the plan you built during calmer times?

You hear about a hot opportunity. Do you evaluate whether it fits your goals, or do you chase momentum because everyone else is excited?

You feel behind financially. Do you speed up and force decisions, or do you slow down and improve execution?

The best decisions are rarely made in emotional moments. They are made through awareness, structure, and discipline.

Athlete Habits and Financial Parallels

Athletes react emotionally to momentum.

Financially, this shows up as panic selling during downturns.

Athletes chase rhythm without discipline.

Financially, this leads to speculation and trend chasing.

Athletes abandon structure when frustrated.

Financially, this creates chaos and inconsistency.

The same habits that lead to rushed shots and blown assignments on the court lead to poor outcomes in investing. Discipline translates across domains.

Time as the Ultimate Advantage

Markets reward three things consistently.

Ownership.

Patience.

Discipline.

You do not need to predict every move. You do not need to time every cycle perfectly. You need to stay invested, rebalance when appropriate, and let time compound effort.

In basketball, great offenses score by trusting spacing and repetition. They know the math works over time. Great investors understand the same truth.

Execution beats excitement.

Process beats prediction.

Consistency beats intensity.

Winning the Long Game

The market is not your opponent.

Emotion is.

Fear.

Greed.

Impatience.

Overconfidence.

Those are the defenders trying to knock you out of rhythm. The solution is not to play faster. It is to play smarter.

Stay invested.

Stick to the plan.

Ignore the noise.

Let time work.

That is how the game slows down.

Athlete Takeaways

Markets exist to connect capital and growth.

Stocks represent ownership. Bonds provide stability.

Volatility is normal, not failure.

Heat checks feel good. Discipline wins.

Stay patient and execute the plan.

The game does not get easier.

You get better at playing it.

Chapter 10: Risk, Return, and the Power of Compounding

Putting In the Reps: Risk, Reward, and the Power of Compounding

Every strength coach teaches the same lesson, whether they say it directly or not.

You do not get stronger from one workout.

You get stronger from showing up consistently, putting in quality reps, allowing your body to recover, and repeating the process over time. Nobody expects visible results after a single lift or conditioning session. Progress feels slow at first. Then, almost without warning, it starts to show up. Strength increases. Movements feel smoother. Confidence grows.

Basketball players understand this intuitively.

Consistency beats intensity.

Money works the same way.

Risk, return, and compounding are not complicated ideas. They are often misunderstood because people expect results too quickly. When progress is not immediate, they assume something is wrong. In reality, the process is working exactly as designed.

Understanding Risk and Reward

There is no reward without risk.

In basketball, attacking the rim creates opportunities. It also invites contact. Taking open shots increases efficiency, but it still comes with misses. Coaches constantly balance risk and reward depending on the game situation, the score, and who is on the floor.

Investing follows the same logic.

Higher potential returns usually come with higher risk. Lower-risk investments tend to be more stable, but they grow more slowly. There is no perfect option that delivers high returns with no downside. Anyone promising that is ignoring reality.

The key is balance.

You do not take contested shots every possession. You do not drive into traffic without spacing. You read the defense and adjust. Smart investing works the same way. Risk should match your situation, your timeline, and your ability to stay disciplined when things get uncomfortable.

Chasing the highest possible return without regard for risk is like jacking shots early in the clock. It might work occasionally, but over time it hurts efficiency and outcomes.

Volatility Is Not the Enemy

This is where many athletes struggle financially.

Volatility is movement.

Permanent loss is damage.

Markets going up and down is normal. That movement can feel uncomfortable, especially when account values drop. Red numbers trigger emotion. They make people feel like something is wrong, even when nothing fundamental has changed.

Volatility alone does not mean failure.

Permanent loss happens when people panic, overextend, or abandon discipline. It happens when they sell at the wrong time, chase risk they do not understand, or take shortcuts to catch up.

In basketball terms, volatility is missing shots. Permanent loss is turning the ball over repeatedly and giving up easy transition points. One is part of the game. The other changes outcomes.

Athletes are trained to respond quickly to discomfort. On the court, that instinct is valuable. Financially, it can lead to mistakes. Feeling uncomfortable does not automatically mean danger. Learning the difference between normal movement and real risk is critical.

Compounding: How Small Wins Add Up

Compounding is growth built on growth.

Your money earns returns.

Those returns earn returns.

Over time, the effect accelerates.

At first, progress looks unimpressive. Then the curve bends. Growth begins to build on itself. This is not magic. It is math combined with time.

Basketball players understand this concept better than most.

One good practice does not change your game.

One good week does not define a season.

But years of quality practices transform skill, conditioning, and confidence. The work compounds. You do not notice it day to day. You notice it when you compare where you started to where you are now.

Money behaves the same way.

The most important ingredient in compounding is time. Not intelligence. Not perfect timing. Time. The earlier you start, the more powerful the effect becomes. This is not because you are smarter. It is because you gave the process more opportunities to work.

Patience matters more than precision.

The Real Cost of Waiting

Waiting feels safe.

People wait to invest until they feel ready. They wait until income increases. They wait until the timing feels right. They wait for clarity, confidence, or certainty.

The problem is that time does not wait with them.

Every year you delay is a year compounding cannot work for you. That lost time cannot be recovered. You can increase contributions later, but you cannot recreate early years of growth.

In basketball terms, skipping offseason training puts you behind before the season even starts. You can still compete, but you are catching up instead of building on momentum.

You do not need to start big.

You do need to start.

Showing up matters more than starting perfectly.

Managing Risk Over Time

Risk is not static. It changes as your life changes.

Early in your career, time is your biggest advantage. Volatility matters less because you have years to recover. As responsibilities increase, risk tolerance often needs adjustment. Families, homes, and career stability change the equation.

This is not about becoming conservative. It is about becoming intentional.

Great teams adjust strategy based on personnel and situation. They do not run the same offense with every lineup. Smart investors do the same. They evolve while staying disciplined.

The mistake is not taking risk.

The mistake is taking risk without understanding it.

A Coach's Perspective

A coach would not complicate this.

Reps matter.

Be consistent.

Trust the process.

Do not cheat the work.

You cannot cram fitness.

You cannot shortcut skill development.

You cannot rush chemistry.

Compounding rewards discipline, not brilliance. Showing up consistently beats occasional intensity every time.

Game Situations and Decision Points

These moments reveal mindset.

The market drops. Do you stop investing or do you keep showing up?

You feel behind financially. Do you force risk or do you stay disciplined?

You want to wait for the perfect moment. Do you start anyway?

The same mindset that wins long seasons wins financially. Professionals stick with the process even when results are not immediately visible.

Athlete Habits and Financial Parallels

Athletes chase quick results.

Financially, this leads to over-risking and impatience.

Athletes skip recovery.

Financially, this shows up as burnout and poor decisions.

Athletes delay preparation.

Financially, this results in lost time that cannot be recovered.

The habits that undermine performance on the court undermine outcomes with money. Discipline translates.

Staying in the Program

Strength gains disappear when training stops.

Skill erodes without repetition.

Conditioning fades without maintenance.

Money works the same way.

Consistency is not exciting.

It is effective.

Staying invested, continuing contributions, rebalancing periodically, and ignoring noise is how progress compounds quietly. The biggest results rarely come from dramatic moves. They come from sustained effort over long periods.

Winning the Long Game

Compounding does not reward excitement.

It rewards consistency.

You do not need to be perfect.

You do not need to time every move.

You do not need to outsmart the system.

You need to show up.

You need to stay patient.

You need to keep putting in reps.

Over time, small decisions stack. What felt insignificant early becomes meaningful later. That is how strength is built. That is how wealth is built.

Athlete Takeaways

Risk and reward always move together.

Volatility is normal. Permanent loss is avoidable.

Compounding rewards patience and repetition.

Waiting costs more than starting imperfectly.

Show up consistently and let time work.

The work compounds even when you are not watching.
Trust the reps.

Chapter 11: Stocks Without the Highlight Reel Hype

Highlights Lie: What Owning Stock Really Means

Every basketball fan loves highlights.

Deep threes from the logo. Posters at the rim. Buzzer beaters that swing seasons. Highlights look incredible in short clips. They are exciting, emotional, and easy to consume. They give the impression that games are decided in a few spectacular moments.

What highlights do not show is everything that actually wins games.

They do not show the spacing that created the driving lane.

They do not show the screen that freed the shooter.

They do not show the extra pass that turned a tough shot into a great one.

They also do not show the missed shots, bad reads, defensive breakdowns, and quiet possessions that slowly lost games.

Stocks get treated the same way.

People talk about massive winners, hot tips, and overnight success stories. Headlines focus on explosive returns and dramatic price moves. Social media rewards bold predictions and flashy outcomes. Very little attention is given to what owning stock actually means, how returns are really created, or why most investors hurt themselves chasing hype instead of building discipline.

This chapter slows the game down.

What Owning Stock Actually Means

Buying a stock is not betting on a ticker symbol.

It is owning a piece of a real business.

When you buy stock, you become a partial owner of a company that sells products or services, pays employees, invests in growth, manages expenses, and tries to generate profit over time. The stock price moves because expectations change, but underneath the price is a real operation with customers, competition, and long-term challenges.

Ownership means participation.

You share in success when the company grows.

You feel pain when it struggles.

You experience volatility along the way.

In basketball terms, owning stock is being on the roster, not just watching highlights. You live with the ups and downs of the season. You do not leave the team because of one bad game. Ownership requires patience, context, and commitment.

If you do not understand what the business does, how it makes money, or why it should exist long term, you are not investing. You are guessing. Guessing can feel exciting. Over time, it usually ends badly.

Why Prices Move and Why That Confuses People

Stock prices move based on expectations, not just results.

Markets constantly try to answer one question. What is this business likely to earn in the future, and how confident are we in that outcome? News, earnings reports, interest rates, innovation, regulation, and competition all influence those expectations.

That is why prices can fall even when a company reports good news.

That is why prices can rise even when current profits are weak.

This disconnect frustrates people who expect stock prices to behave logically in the short term. Basketball teaches you something similar. A team can play well and still lose. A bad shooting night does not always reflect bad execution. Context matters.

The market is not irrational.

It is forward-looking.

Growth and Value: Different Roles, Same Goal

Two common approaches to stock investing are growth and value. Neither is right or wrong. They simply play different roles.

Growth investing focuses on companies expected to expand quickly. These businesses reinvest heavily, prioritize scale, and often trade at higher prices because investors expect strong future growth. The upside can be significant. So can the volatility.

Value investing focuses on companies priced lower relative to their fundamentals. These businesses may grow more slowly, operate in mature industries, or be temporarily out of favor. They often provide more stability and sometimes income, but they rarely feel exciting.

In basketball terms, growth stocks are fast-break teams.

They push pace.

They score in bunches.

They thrive on momentum.

They can look unstoppable.

Value stocks are half-court teams.

They execute.

They control tempo.

They rely on fundamentals.

They win quietly.

Both approaches can succeed. Problems arise when expectations are misaligned. When you expect a half-court team to play like a fast-break team, frustration follows. The same happens when investors panic because a value stock is not exciting or a growth stock experiences volatility.

Smart investors understand roles. They build portfolios with balance, not bias. They do not demand every holding perform the same function.

Dividends and the Reality of Total Return

Dividends confuse many athletes.

Dividends are cash payments companies make to shareholders. They often get framed as free money or passive income. In reality, dividends are simply one component of total return.

Total return includes three things.

Changes in the stock price.

Dividends paid.

Reinvestment of earnings.

When a company pays a dividend, that cash comes from the business itself. The value does not appear out of nowhere. It is distributed from profits that could have been reinvested instead.

In basketball terms, total return is the final score.

Points alone do not tell the story.

Defense matters.

Assists matter.

Efficiency matters.

Focusing only on dividends or only on price appreciation misses the bigger picture. What matters is how all components work together over time. A disciplined approach to total return beats chasing any single metric.

The Highlight Trap in Investing

The biggest danger in stock investing is mistaking excitement for effectiveness.

Highlight culture trains people to believe that success comes from big moments. In basketball, that mindset leads to forced shots and hero ball. In investing, it leads to hype chasing and poor timing.

People hear about the stock that doubled.

They ignore the dozens that failed.

They enter late.

They exit early.

They repeat the cycle.

Most investors do not lose money because markets are rigged. They lose money because they abandon discipline in search of excitement.

Ownership rewards patience.

Speculation rewards emotion.

Emotion is expensive.

Common Investing Myths That Refuse to Die

Several myths show up again and again.

Myth: Stocks are gambling.

Reality: Ownership with discipline is investing. Guessing without understanding is gambling.

Myth: You need to pick winners to succeed.

Reality: Consistent exposure, diversification, and time matter far more than individual picks.

Myth: You must be aggressive to win.

Reality: Forcing shots lowers efficiency. Patience compounds results.

Myth: You can time the market.

Reality: Most people cannot. Trying often reduces returns.

These myths persist because they are simple and emotional. Basketball teaches you to respect fundamentals even when the crowd wants highlights. Investing demands the same discipline.

A Coach's Perspective

A coach would say this clearly.

Know your role.

Play within the system.

Do not chase highlights.

Let the game come to you.

Coaches understand that winning is boring up close. It is repetition, spacing, communication, and trust. Flashy moments are a byproduct, not the strategy.

Stocks reward discipline, not flash.

Game Situations and Decision Points

Every investor faces these moments.

You hear about a hot stock. Do you research the business or chase momentum because others are excited?

A stock you own drops. Do you panic, or do you reassess whether the business fundamentals changed?

You feel bored. Do you sacrifice discipline for entertainment?

These are possession-level decisions. Individually, they seem small. Over time, they compound into meaningful outcomes.

Athlete Habits and Financial Parallels

Athletes chase highlights.

Financially, that leads to hype-driven investing.

Athletes ignore roles.

Financially, that leads to unbalanced portfolios.

Athletes overreact to mistakes.

Financially, that leads to buying high and selling low.

The habits that hurt performance on the court hurt results in the market. Fundamentals translate everywhere.

Winning Without the Spotlight

Most successful investors never feel exciting.

They rebalance.

They stay diversified.

They ignore noise.

They remain patient.

They understand that markets reward ownership, discipline, and time.

You do not need perfect timing. You need consistency and restraint.

Basketball games are not won on highlights alone. Championships are built on fundamentals executed repeatedly under pressure.

Investment results are no different.

Athlete Takeaways

Owning stock means owning a real business.

Growth and value play different roles. Respect both.

Dividends are part of total return, not a shortcut.

Hype creates mistakes. Discipline creates results.

Stay patient and play the long game.

Highlights look great.

Fundamentals win seasons.

Chapter 12: Bonds and Playing Solid Half-Court Defense

Half-Court Defense: Why Bonds Matter When the Game Slows Down

Not every possession is a fast break.

Championship teams know how to score in transition. They run when opportunities are there. They push pace after steals, long rebounds, and bad shots. But they also know something just as important. When the game slows down, when shots stop falling, and when momentum swings the wrong way, half-court defense keeps you alive.

Teams that rely only on speed and scoring eventually get exposed. When legs get tired. When whistles tighten. When emotions rise. That is when structure matters. That is when discipline matters. That is when defense wins possessions quietly and consistently.

Bonds play that role in a portfolio.

They are not exciting. They do not dominate conversations. They rarely produce dramatic stories. But when conditions get tough, bonds provide structure, stability, and reliability. Understanding bonds helps you appreciate why defense matters just as much as offense in your financial life.

What a Bond Really Is

A bond is a loan.

When you buy a bond, you are lending money to a borrower. That borrower might be a government, a city, or a company. In exchange for that loan, the borrower agrees to pay you interest and return your principal at a specified time, assuming they do not default.

That is it.

There is no mystery. There is no speculation about ownership. You are not buying growth. You are providing capital and being compensated for it.

In basketball terms, bonds are defensive possessions.

You are not looking for explosive upside.

You are not chasing momentum.

You are controlling the game.

You are limiting mistakes.

You are protecting position.

The value of bonds can move in the market, but that movement is not their primary purpose. Bonds are designed to provide income, stability, and predictability. They exist to reduce volatility, not create excitement.

Why Bonds Feel Boring and Why That Is the Point

Many athletes struggle with bonds because bonds feel boring.

There are no highlights.

There are no big swings.

There is no adrenaline rush.

But boredom is often a sign that something is working exactly as intended.

In basketball, great defense rarely shows up on the stat sheet. It shows up in missed shots, rushed decisions, and broken rhythm for the opponent. The casual fan may not notice it, but coaches do. Teammates do. Winning teams absolutely do.

Bonds work the same way.

They quietly do their job.

They reduce stress.

They provide consistency.

They create space for offense to operate.

A portfolio with no bonds is relying entirely on offense. Sometimes that works. Over long seasons and long markets, it usually creates unnecessary risk.

The Two Main Risks in Bonds

Bonds are not risk-free. They are simply different kinds of risk.

Two primary risks affect bonds.

Interest Rate Risk

Interest rate risk means bond prices move when interest rates change.

When interest rates rise, existing bonds with lower rates become less attractive, so their prices fall. When interest rates fall, existing bonds with higher rates become more valuable, so their prices rise.

This movement confuses people who expect bonds to never fluctuate. But the purpose of bonds is not to eliminate movement. It is to reduce overall volatility and provide income.

In basketball terms, interest rate risk is pace.

A faster pace changes shot selection.

A slower pace changes spacing.

The game still functions, but adjustments matter.

Credit Risk

Credit risk is the risk that the borrower cannot repay the loan.

Governments with strong finances tend to have lower credit risk. Companies with weaker balance sheets carry higher credit risk. Higher credit risk usually comes with higher interest payments as compensation.

In basketball terms, credit risk is matchup.

Some matchups are safe.

Some require help.

Some need adjustments.

Strong teams manage matchups by understanding strengths and weaknesses. Smart investors manage credit risk by diversifying and not overreaching for yield.

Higher yield almost always means higher risk. There is no free lunch. Defense still requires discipline.

Why Bond Prices Move Even When Nothing Feels Wrong

One of the most confusing experiences for new investors is seeing bond values move even when nothing dramatic seems to be happening.

Interest rates change.

Inflation expectations shift.

Economic outlooks evolve.

Bond prices respond quietly and constantly. This movement is not a sign that bonds are broken. It is the system adjusting to new information.

In basketball, defensive adjustments happen possession by possession. You do not notice them unless you are looking closely. But over time, they change outcomes.

Bond movement is similar. It is subtle. It is contextual. It is not meant to be dramatic.

When Bonds Make Sense

Bonds make the most sense when stability matters.

As income grows.

As responsibilities increase.

As timelines shorten.

As flexibility becomes important.

If you need money in the near future, bonds help reduce the risk that market volatility forces bad decisions. If you are approaching a goal with a defined timeline, bonds help preserve capital.

If your career is just starting and time is on your side, bonds may play a smaller role. That does not mean zero role. It means intentional role.

In basketball terms, this is lineup management.

Young, athletic teams run more.

Veteran teams slow the game down.

Both approaches can win when used correctly.

The mistake is not using bonds.

The mistake is ignoring context.

Bonds as a Shock Absorber

One of the most important functions of bonds is emotional.

Bonds reduce volatility.

Reduced volatility reduces panic.

Reduced panic improves decision-making.

This matters more than people realize.

Many investors do not fail because of poor strategy. They fail because volatility pushes them into emotional decisions. Bonds act as a shock absorber. They help keep portfolios functional when markets get rough.

In basketball terms, bonds are the glue players.

They may not score much.

They may not lead in highlights.

But they communicate.

They rotate.

They keep the team connected.

Without glue players, talent falls apart under pressure. Without bonds, portfolios often do the same.

Diversification and Balance

A diversified portfolio needs offense and defense.

Stocks drive growth.

Bonds provide stability.

Cash provides flexibility.

Each has a role. None should be evaluated in isolation.

Ignoring bonds completely is like playing five scorers and hoping nothing goes wrong. It might work in short bursts. Over long seasons, it creates exposure.

Balance is not about playing scared.

It is about playing smart.

A Coach's Perspective

A coach would remind you of a few truths.

Defense travels.

Control the tempo.

Protect the lead.

Do not force the game.

Great coaches know that offense comes and goes. Defense keeps you competitive even when shots do not fall. Bonds help you do the same financially.

They allow you to stay invested.

They allow you to avoid panic.

They allow you to play the long game.

Game Situations and Decision Points

These moments reveal understanding.

Markets are volatile. Do you panic or lean on stability?

You need funds soon. Do you chase returns or protect capital?

You want balance. Do you respect defense or ignore it?

Smart decisions come from understanding roles, not reacting to emotion.

Athlete Habits and Financial Parallels

Athletes undervalue defense.

Financially, that shows up as ignoring bonds.

Athletes chase speed constantly.

Financially, that means taking too much risk.

Athletes lose situational awareness.

Financially, that leads to poor timing and forced decisions.

The habits that lose games late also damage financial outcomes. Discipline translates.

Winning When Conditions Get Tough

You do not win championships on offense alone.

Defense keeps you alive when the game gets tight. It keeps you competitive when momentum swings. It buys time for offense to recover.

Bonds play that same role in your financial life.

They slow the game down.

They reduce mistakes.

They give you options.

They protect flexibility.

They are not exciting.

They are effective.

Athlete Takeaways

Bonds are loans designed for stability.

Interest rate risk and credit risk both matter.

Bonds fit best when timelines shorten or stability becomes important.

Defense balances offense in a portfolio.

Solid half-court defense wins long games.

Fast breaks are fun.
Defense wins seasons.

Chapter 13: Funds, ETFs, and Team Basketball Investing

Team Basketball: Why Funds and ETFs Win Over Long Seasons

Great basketball is rarely about one player doing everything. Championship teams move the ball. They trust spacing. They understand timing. Each player knows their role and executes it consistently. When the ball finds the open man, efficiency rises and mistakes drop. When someone tries to play hero every possession, the offense stagnates. Turnovers increase. Shot quality falls. Even talented teams lose games this way.

Funds and ETFs work the same way in investing.

They are team basketball for your money. Instead of relying on one stock, one idea, or one prediction, you spread responsibility across many players. That approach reduces risk, increases consistency, and keeps you competitive over long seasons.

This chapter is about understanding why boring often wins, why systems beat isolation, and why discipline matters more than excitement.

Why Team Investing Matters

Most people think investing is about finding the right stock.

The perfect company.

The next breakout.

The one idea that changes everything.

That mindset mirrors pickup basketball. One player dominates the ball. Everyone else watches. It looks impressive in moments. Over time, it fails.

Markets reward process, not hero ball.

When you rely on a single stock, you are betting that one business, one management team, one industry, and one moment in time will deliver everything you need. Sometimes that works. More often, it creates unnecessary risk.

Funds and ETFs solve this problem by spreading responsibility.

One fund can own hundreds or even thousands of companies.

No single mistake can derail the entire plan.

No single win needs to carry the team.

That is team basketball.

Mutual Funds and ETFs: Same Concept, Different Pace

Both mutual funds and ETFs pool money from many investors and invest it across multiple securities. Stocks, bonds, or a mix of both. The goal is diversification and efficiency.

The difference lies in how they operate.

Mutual funds are typically bought and sold once per day. Everyone transacts at the same price after the market closes. This structure encourages patience and long-term thinking. There is no temptation to react to intraday noise.

ETFs trade throughout the day like stocks. Prices move in real time. That flexibility can be useful, but it can also invite unnecessary tinkering if discipline slips.

In basketball terms, both run organized systems.

Mutual funds are half-court teams.

They slow the game down.

They emphasize execution.

They limit impulsive decisions.

ETFs offer more flexibility.

They can adjust quickly.

They allow more tactical movement.

Neither is inherently better.

The wrong question is which one is superior.

The right question is which one fits how you execute.

The wrapper matters far less than what is inside.

What Is Inside the Jersey Matters Most

A fund or ETF is only as good as its underlying holdings.

Some own large companies.

Some own small companies.

Some focus on growth.

Some focus on value.

Some invest domestically.

Some invest globally.

Some focus on income.

Some focus on stability.

Choosing a fund without understanding what it owns is like recruiting players without knowing their skill set. Names do not win games. Fit does.

The goal is not complexity.

The goal is role clarity.

Index Strategies: Running a Proven System

Index strategies aim to match the performance of a specific market or segment of the market.

They follow rules.

They do not guess.

They do not react emotionally.

They keep costs low.

Index investing is not about brilliance. It is about consistency.

In basketball terms, index investing is running a proven system.

The plays are known.

The spacing is defined.

The expectations are clear.

You are not trying to outsmart anyone. You are executing something that has worked over time. That simplicity is powerful.

Most long-term investors benefit from building their portfolio around a core index strategy. It provides broad exposure, diversification, and predictability. It reduces the need for constant decisions.

Systems reduce mistakes.

Active Strategies: Playmaking Requires Skill

Active strategies attempt to outperform the market through selection and timing.

Managers analyze companies.

They make bets.

They adjust positions.

They try to add value through judgment.

Active investing is like trusting individual playmaking.

When it works, it looks great.

When it fails, it is obvious.

The challenge is consistency. Outperforming the market repeatedly over time is extremely difficult. Even skilled professionals struggle to do it year after year.

This does not mean active strategies are bad.

It means they require discipline, realistic expectations, and careful use.

Many investors make the mistake of expecting active strategies to deliver highlights every night. That is not how basketball works, and it is not how markets work.

Most people are better served building around a core system and using active strategies sparingly, if at all.

Fees: The Quiet Stat That Changes Games

Fees matter more than most people realize.

Every fund and ETF charges an expense ratio. That fee comes out of returns every year. It does not matter whether markets are up or down. The fee is paid regardless.

Small percentages feel harmless.

Over time, they are not.

Fees compound against you.

In basketball terms, fees are turnovers.

One turnover does not lose a game.

Five extra turnovers every night change seasons.

Low costs do not guarantee success.

High costs make success harder.

A disciplined investor pays attention to efficiency, just like a disciplined coach values shot selection and ball security.

Diversification Without Overcomplication

Diversification is often misunderstood.

It does not mean owning everything.

It does not mean endless funds.

It does not mean confusion.

Diversification means spreading risk intelligently.

Different companies.

Different industries.

Different regions.

Different roles.

Funds and ETFs make this simple.

One fund can give exposure to an entire market.
One portfolio can balance growth and stability.
One strategy can cover multiple outcomes.
In basketball terms, this is roster construction.
You do not need five superstars.
You need players who complement each other.
Too much overlap creates inefficiency.
Too little balance creates risk.
The goal is cohesion.

Why Simplicity Wins

Complexity feels sophisticated.

Simplicity performs.

The more moving parts you introduce, the more opportunities for mistakes. Funds and ETFs reduce the need for constant decisions. They allow you to focus on contribution, discipline, and patience.

This matters more than intelligence.

This matters more than predictions.

Execution wins.

A Coach's Perspective

A coach would keep it simple.

Trust the system.

Share the ball.

Know your role.

Win together.

Isolation basketball is exhausting.

Team basketball is sustainable.

Funds and ETFs allow you to invest like a team. They reduce ego. They reduce emotion. They reward consistency.

Game Situations and Decision Points

These are the moments that define outcomes.

You want simplicity. Do you choose diversification or chase individual names?

You hear about a high-fee product. Do you evaluate cost or get distracted by promises?

You want consistency. Do you trust a system or force plays?

The same principles that win games win financially.

Athlete Habits and Financial Parallels

Athletes rely on individual talent.

Financially, that shows up as concentrated risk.

Athletes ignore efficiency.

Financially, that shows up as high fees.

Athletes complicate execution.

Financially, that leads to confusion and inconsistency.

Fundamentals translate.

Winning Over Long Seasons

Championships are not won by highlight reels alone.

They are won by teams that execute every night, limit mistakes, and trust the process when things get uncomfortable. Funds and ETFs support that mindset.

They allow you to invest with discipline.

They reduce unnecessary risk.

They help you stay consistent.

You do not need to be perfect.

You need to stay in the game.

Athlete Takeaways

Funds and ETFs spread risk across a team.

Index strategies offer consistency and low cost.

Active strategies require skill and discipline.

Fees quietly reduce performance over time.

Diversification keeps you competitive.

Team basketball is not flashy.

It wins championships.

So does disciplined investing.

Chapter 14: Real Estate and Alternative Plays

Playing in the Paint: Real Estate and Alternatives Without Losing Mobility

Not every possession ends with a jump shot.

Some games are won in transition. Others are won by spacing and ball movement. And some games are decided in the paint through physical play, patience, and control of space. Great teams understand that interior play is powerful, but only when used at the right time. Forcing the ball inside when the defense is set leads to turnovers. Ignoring the paint entirely leaves easy points on the table.

Real estate and alternative investments are the interior plays of your financial life.

They can create strength.

They can create leverage.

They can also slow you down if you do not understand the trade-offs.

This chapter is not about selling real estate or alternatives as must-have strategies. It is about understanding when they fit, when they do not, and how to use them without sacrificing flexibility.

Renting and Owning Are Tools, Not Identities

Renting and owning are often framed as moral choices or milestones of success. That framing causes people to make poor decisions.

Renting and owning serve different purposes.

Renting offers flexibility.

Lower upfront costs.

Easier relocation.

Fewer unexpected expenses.

Less responsibility for repairs and maintenance.

Owning offers stability.

Potential appreciation.

Forced savings through mortgage payments.

Control over the space you live in.

In basketball terms, renting is playing light and fast. You can change direction quickly. You are not committed to one spot on the floor. Owning is setting your feet in the post. You establish position and absorb contact, but movement becomes slower.

Neither approach is superior on its own.

The right choice depends on your stage of life, income stability, geographic plans, and priorities. A young professional with uncertain job location may benefit from renting longer. Someone with stable income and long-term plans may benefit from owning.

Buying too early or too aggressively can limit flexibility. Repairs, taxes, insurance, and market conditions add friction. Selling is not instant. Renting longer than needed can delay progress if stability is already present.

The goal is fit, not status.

The Hidden Responsibilities of Ownership

Many people focus on the upside of owning and underestimate the responsibility.

Mortgage payments are only part of the cost.

Maintenance is ongoing.

Unexpected repairs happen.

Property taxes change.

Insurance costs rise.

Markets fluctuate.

Owning a home is not just an investment. It is an operating business that requires cash flow and attention.

In basketball terms, posting up requires conditioning and awareness. You cannot just catch the ball and expect success. You have to feel the defender, read help defense, and know when to kick it out.

Ownership rewards preparation.

It punishes assumptions.

Real Estate Does Not Require Being a Landlord

One of the biggest misconceptions about real estate is that it requires hands-on management.

It does not.

Real Estate Investment Trusts, commonly called REITs, allow investors to own shares of income-producing real estate without managing tenants, repairs, or financing. REITs can own apartments, office buildings, warehouses, data centers, healthcare facilities, and more.

They trade like stocks.

They provide income.

They offer diversification.

They remain liquid.

In basketball terms, REITs are off-ball contributions.

You are still part of the play.

You still benefit from movement.

You do not need to handle the ball every possession.

REITs allow exposure to real estate while preserving simplicity and flexibility. They can be especially useful for investors who want real estate exposure without the operational burden.

Indirect ownership is not lesser ownership. It is simply a different role.

Alternatives and the Allure of Complexity

Alternative investments include assets outside traditional stocks and bonds.

Commodities.

Private equity.

Private credit.

Hedge strategies.

Other nontraditional investments.

These options are often marketed as sophisticated, exclusive, or superior. They promise diversification or higher returns. Sometimes they deliver. Often they come with trade-offs that are not fully understood.

Higher fees.

Less transparency.

Longer lockups.

Limited liquidity.

Complex structures.

In basketball terms, alternatives are specialty plays.

They can work.

They can surprise defenses.

They can also stall the offense if overused or misunderstood.

Specialty plays are situational. They are not the foundation of the playbook. The fundamentals still matter most.

Complexity is not the same as advantage.

Liquidity Is a Strategic Asset

Liquidity is how easily you can access your money.

Stocks and bonds are generally liquid.

You can sell them quickly.

You can rebalance.

You can adjust.

Real estate and many alternatives are illiquid.

Selling takes time.

Prices are uncertain.

Access may be limited.

Liquidity matters more than people realize.

Illiquid investments reduce flexibility. They can force bad decisions if cash is needed unexpectedly. Emergencies, career changes, family needs, or opportunities require access to capital.

In basketball terms, liquidity is spacing.

When the floor is spaced well, options exist.

When the floor is clogged, choices disappear.

Liquidity creates space.

Space creates options.

Options create control.

When Interior Play Makes Sense

Interior play is powerful when the situation fits.

Stable income.

Adequate emergency reserves.

Long time horizon.

Clear understanding of risk.

Comfort with reduced flexibility.

When these elements are present, real estate and alternatives can add strength to a portfolio. They can diversify income sources. They can reduce reliance on public markets. They can provide different forms of return.

When these elements are missing, interior play becomes forced.

Forcing a post-up against a double team leads to turnovers. Forcing illiquid investments before readiness leads to stress and regret.

Context matters.

The Psychological Side of Illiquidity

Illiquidity affects more than finances. It affects behavior.

When money is locked up, people feel trapped.

When access is limited, anxiety increases.

When options disappear, mistakes compound.

Many investors overestimate their tolerance for illiquidity during calm periods. Stress reveals the truth.

In basketball, fatigue exposes weaknesses. Financial pressure does the same.

Understanding yourself matters as much as understanding the investment.

A Coach's Perspective

A coach would emphasize awareness.

Know the situation.

Do not force the post.

Use the right play at the right time.

Protect flexibility.

Read the defense.

Interior play is powerful when used intentionally. It is damaging when used out of ego or impatience.

Game Situations and Decision Points

These moments define outcomes.

You want to buy property. Do you evaluate fit or chase status?

You want diversification. Do you understand liquidity trade-offs or just hear the upside?

You hear about a private deal. Do you understand the lockup, fees, and risks?

These are not emotional decisions. They are situational ones.

Athlete Habits and Financial Parallels

Athletes chase physicality at the wrong time.

Financially, that means illiquid investments too early.

Athletes overestimate strength.

Financially, that means underestimating risk and leverage.

Athletes confuse complexity with skill.

Financially, that leads to overcomplicated portfolios.

The habits that create turnovers in the paint create financial stress off the court.

Using Strength Without Losing Movement

Real estate and alternatives are not shortcuts.

They require patience.

They require capital.

They require understanding.

They require discipline.

Used well, they add strength.

Used poorly, they limit movement.

Great teams know when to slow the game down and when to speed it up. Great investors do the same.

Winning With Awareness

Interior play wins championships when used correctly.

It creates high-percentage opportunities.

It controls tempo.

It wears down opponents.

But it only works when the fundamentals are in place and the timing is right.

Financially, the same rules apply.

Athlete Takeaways

Renting and owning serve different stages and goals.

REITs offer real estate exposure without hands-on responsibility.

Alternatives require discipline and understanding.

Liquidity creates flexibility under pressure.

Use interior plays when the situation fits.

Strength matters.

So does mobility.

Championships require both.

Part IV: Managing the Season (Portfolio Management)

Championships are won through adjustments, not ego.

No basketball season goes exactly as planned.

Roles change. Injuries happen. Matchups evolve. What worked in November may not work in March. The teams that last are not the ones with the best preseason predictions. They are the ones that adjust without panicking and stay disciplined without getting stubborn.

Portfolio management is the long season of investing.

Building a portfolio is one thing. Managing it over time is where results are actually determined. This part of the playbook is about staying engaged without overreacting. Making smart adjustments without abandoning the plan. Letting discipline, not ego, guide decisions.

Ego shows up when players force shots to prove something. It shows up financially when people chase performance, refuse to admit mistakes, or react emotionally to short-term outcomes. Adjustments require humility. They require awareness. They require the ability to separate identity from results.

Great teams watch film continuously.

They evaluate what is working.

They recognize what has changed.

They make adjustments based on reality, not hope.

Great investors do the same.

This section focuses on asset allocation, buying and holding with discipline, reviewing progress, and making halftime adjustments when life changes. It also addresses the mental side of money, because mindset determines whether adjustments are thoughtful or reactionary.

Managing the season does not mean constant tinkering. It means knowing when to act and when to stay put. It means understanding that staying the course is sometimes the hardest adjustment of all.

The goal is not perfection.

The goal is resilience.

Championships are not won by the team that never faces adversity. They are won by the team that responds to it correctly.

That is how portfolios are managed.

Chapter 15: Asset Allocation: Building the Right Rotation

Setting the Rotation: Why Asset Allocation Drives Everything Else

No championship team plays the same five players every minute. Rotations exist for a reason. Matchups change. Fatigue accumulates. Roles matter. Coaches manage minutes not because their starters are weak, but because balance over time wins. A lineup that looks great in short stretches can break down over a full game or a long season if it is not supported correctly.

Asset allocation is your financial rotation.

It determines how much offense, defense, and flexibility you have at any given moment. When the rotation fits, the game flows. When it does not, even strong individual investments struggle to work together.

This chapter is not about finding the perfect asset. It is about building a lineup that can function across different conditions.

Stocks, Bonds, and Cash: Understanding the Roles

Every portfolio is built on three core components.

Stocks drive growth.

Bonds provide stability and income.

Cash provides flexibility and protection.

Each plays a distinct role. None is optional. Problems arise when one role dominates at the expense of the others.

In basketball terms, stocks are your scorers. They push the offense. They create momentum. They also miss shots and experience cold streaks. That is normal.

Bonds are your defenders. They slow the game down. They protect leads. They do not generate excitement, but they keep you competitive when conditions tighten.

Cash is your sixth man. It does not start every game, but when something unexpected happens, it is ready. Cash allows adjustments without forcing bad decisions. It creates optionality.

Too much offense without defense creates volatility. Too much defense without offense limits progress. Too much cash without a plan leads to stagnation. Balance creates consistency.

Domestic and International Exposure: Expanding the Court

Limiting investments to one country is like playing only one style of basketball.

The global economy includes different growth rates, demographics, industries, and cycles. While markets are connected, they do not move in perfect sync. International exposure reduces reliance on a single system.

In basketball terms, this is scouting beyond your conference. You broaden your talent pool. You gain flexibility. You avoid putting all your success in one matchup.

Global diversification does not eliminate volatility. It spreads it. That matters more than most people realize. When one region struggles, another may hold steady or recover faster.

Diversification is not about predicting which country will win. It is about reducing dependency.

What Diversification Actually Means

Diversification is often misunderstood.

It does not mean owning everything.

It does not mean endless complexity.

It does not mean collecting investments.

Diversification means spreading risk intelligently.

Different assets respond differently to inflation, interest rates, growth, and stress. Stocks, bonds, real estate, and cash all behave differently under pressure. When combined thoughtfully, they reduce the chance that one event derails the entire plan.

In basketball terms, diversification is lineup versatility.

You do not ask one player to score, defend, rebound, and organize the offense every possession. You build a roster that can adapt. When one option is taken away, another steps up.

Concentration increases risk.

Diversification increases durability.

How Age and Career Stage Change the Rotation

Rotations evolve over time.

Early in your career, time is your biggest advantage. Volatility matters less because recovery time is long. Growth assets often play a larger role. The focus is development, not protection.

As income grows and responsibilities increase, stability becomes more important. Families, mortgages, and career risk change the equation. The rotation adjusts. Defense and flexibility matter more.

In basketball terms, young teams run more.

Veteran teams value efficiency and control.

Neither approach is better. They are situational.

The mistake is freezing the rotation. Asset allocation is not static. It should evolve as your life evolves. What made sense at 25 may not make sense at 45. What worked during accumulation may not work during distribution.

Adaptation is not weakness. It is awareness.

Why Asset Allocation Matters More Than Selection

Many people obsess over individual investments.

The right stock.

The perfect fund.

The next opportunity.

In reality, asset allocation drives most long-term outcomes. Getting the mix right matters far more than picking a single winner.

A great scorer in the wrong lineup struggles.

An average player in the right system thrives.

Asset allocation determines how your investments interact under stress. It controls volatility, behavior, and sustainability. It is the framework everything else operates within.

A Coach's Perspective

A coach would focus on balance.

Know your personnel.

Manage minutes.

Adjust for matchups.

Think long term.

Great coaches do not chase short-term runs at the expense of the season. They protect players so they are available when it matters most.

Rotations win championships.

So does disciplined asset allocation.

Game Situations and Decision Points

These moments test the rotation.

You feel confident and want more risk. Does your lineup support that, or are you already overextended?

Life changes. New job. New family responsibilities. Do you adjust the rotation or keep forcing the same lineup?

Markets move sharply. Do you react emotionally or trust the structure you built?

The right rotation supports execution under pressure. The wrong one amplifies mistakes.

Athlete Habits and Financial Parallels

Athletes overplay starters.

Financially, that shows up as overconcentration.

Athletes ignore matchups.

Financially, that leads to poor allocation.

Athletes resist rotation changes.

Financially, that results in outdated strategies.

What costs games late also costs results over time.

Winning Over Long Seasons

Asset allocation is not about predicting the future.

It is about preparing for many versions of it.

When the rotation fits, decisions become easier. Volatility becomes manageable. Discipline becomes sustainable.

Get the rotation right, and execution improves everywhere else.

Athlete Takeaways

Stocks, bonds, and cash all play distinct roles.

Balance creates consistency.

Diversification spreads risk.

Asset allocation should evolve with your life.

Smart rotations win long seasons.

Talent matters.

Structure matters more.

Chapter 16: Buying, Holding, and Trusting the Game Plan

Setting the Rotation: Why Asset Allocation Drives Everything Else

No championship team plays the same five players every minute. Rotations exist for a reason. Matchups change. Fatigue builds. Roles matter. Coaches manage minutes not because their starters are weak, but because balance over time wins. A lineup that looks great for short stretches can break down over a full game or an entire season if it is not supported correctly.

Asset allocation is your financial rotation.

It determines how much offense, defense, and flexibility you have at any given moment. When the rotation fits, the game flows. When it does not, even strong individual investments struggle to work together. This chapter is not about finding the perfect asset. It is about building a lineup that can function across different conditions.

Stocks, Bonds, and Cash: Understanding the Roles

Every portfolio is built on three core components.

Stocks drive growth.

Bonds provide stability and income.

Cash provides flexibility and protection.

Each has a specific role. None is optional. Problems arise when one dominates at the expense of the others.

In basketball terms, stocks are your scorers. They push the offense and create momentum. They also miss shots and go through cold stretches. That is part of the game.

Bonds are your defenders. They slow things down, protect leads, and keep you competitive when conditions tighten. They are rarely exciting, but they prevent the game from getting out of control.

Cash is your sixth man. It may not start, but it is always ready. Cash allows adjustments without forcing bad decisions. It creates options when circumstances change.

Too much offense without defense creates volatility. Too much defense without offense limits progress. Too much cash without a plan leads to stagnation. Balance creates consistency.

Domestic and International Exposure: Expanding the Court

Limiting investments to one country is like playing only one style of basketball.

The global economy includes different growth rates, demographics, industries, and cycles. While markets are connected, they do not move in perfect sync. International exposure reduces reliance on any single system.

In basketball terms, this is scouting beyond your conference. You expand your options. You reduce dependency on one matchup. You give yourself more ways to win.

Global diversification does not eliminate volatility. It spreads it. That matters more than most people realize. When one region struggles, another may hold steady or recover faster.

This is not about predicting which country will outperform. It is about reducing concentration risk.

What Diversification Actually Means

Diversification is often misunderstood.

It does not mean owning everything.

It does not mean endless complexity.

It does not mean collecting investments.

Diversification means spreading risk intelligently.

Different assets respond differently to inflation, interest rates, growth, and stress. Stocks, bonds, real estate, and cash behave differently under pressure. When combined thoughtfully, they reduce the chance that one event derails the entire plan.

In basketball terms, diversification is lineup versatility.

You do not ask one player to score, defend, rebound, and organize the offense every possession. You build a roster that can adjust. When one option is taken away, another steps in.

Concentration increases risk.

Diversification increases durability.

How Age and Career Stage Change the Rotation

Rotations evolve over time.

Early in your career, time is your biggest advantage. Volatility matters less because recovery time is long. Growth assets often play a larger role. The focus is development, not protection.

As income grows and responsibilities increase, stability becomes more important. Families, mortgages, and career risk change the equation. The rotation adjusts. Defense and flexibility matter more.

In basketball terms, young teams run more.

Veteran teams value efficiency and control.

Neither approach is better. They are situational.

The mistake is freezing the rotation. Asset allocation is not static. It should evolve as your life evolves. What made sense at 25 may not make sense at 45. What worked during accumulation may not work during distribution.

Adaptation is not weakness. It is awareness.

Why Asset Allocation Matters More Than Selection

Many people obsess over individual investments.

The right stock.

The perfect fund.

The next opportunity.

In reality, asset allocation drives most long-term outcomes. Getting the mix right matters far more than picking a single winner.

A great scorer in the wrong lineup struggles.

An average player in the right system thrives.

Asset allocation determines how your investments interact under stress. It controls volatility, behavior, and sustainability. It is the framework everything else operates within.

A Coach's Perspective

A coach would focus on balance.

Know your personnel.

Manage minutes.

Adjust for matchups.

Think long term.

Great coaches do not chase short-term runs at the expense of the season. They protect players so they are available when it matters most.

Rotations win championships.

So does disciplined asset allocation.

Game Situations and Decision Points

These moments test the rotation.

You feel confident and want more risk. Does your lineup support that, or are you already overextended?

Life changes. New job. New family responsibilities. Do you adjust the rotation or keep forcing the same lineup?

Markets move sharply. Do you react emotionally or trust the structure you built?

The right rotation supports execution under pressure. The wrong one amplifies mistakes.

Winning Over Long Seasons

Asset allocation is not about predicting the future.

It is about preparing for many versions of it.

When the rotation fits, decisions become easier. Volatility becomes manageable. Discipline becomes sustainable. Get the rotation right, and execution improves everywhere else.

Athlete Takeaways

Stocks, bonds, and cash all play distinct roles.

Balance creates consistency.

Diversification spreads risk.

Asset allocation should evolve with your life.

Smart rotations win long seasons.

Talent matters.

Structure matters more.

If you want, next we can:

- tighten this further for audiobook pacing
- add a short "locker room summary" version
- align this chapter with a CFP-style framework
- transition cleanly into the next chapter

Just tell me where you want to go next.

Chapter 17: Rebalancing and Halftime Adjustments

Halftime exists for a reason.

It is not a panic session.

It is not a time to tear everything down.

It is a moment to step back, review the film, and make smart adjustments.

Good teams understand this. They do not chase the last few possessions. They do not let emotion dictate strategy. They evaluate what is working, what has drifted, and what needs correction. Then they make changes with purpose.

Rebalancing serves the same role in your financial life.

Markets move. Asset values shift. Over time, even a well-built portfolio drifts away from its original rotation. Rebalancing brings it back into alignment without emotion. It restores structure instead of reacting to noise.

How Often to Review Investments

You do not check the scoreboard every possession.

Constant monitoring creates anxiety. Every market move feels urgent. Short-term swings start to look like signals instead of normal movement. That leads to rushed decisions.

At the same time, ignoring your portfolio entirely allows small problems to grow unnoticed.

Most investors benefit from scheduled reviews, not constant attention.

Annual or semiannual check-ins are usually enough. The purpose is awareness, not micromanagement. You are checking alignment, not chasing performance.

In basketball terms, this is film study.

You review film to improve execution, not to relive every missed shot or bad call. You look for patterns. You identify drift. You make corrections calmly.

Too much watching creates noise. Too little creates blind spots. Discipline lives in the middle.

What Rebalancing Really Means

Rebalancing means adjusting your portfolio back to its intended allocation.

If stocks perform well for an extended period, they grow into a larger portion of the portfolio. Risk increases quietly. Bonds and cash shrink relative to the original plan.

Rebalancing trims what has grown and adds to what has lagged. It restores balance.

This feels counterintuitive.

It means selling assets that have performed well and adding to assets that have underperformed. Emotion pushes investors to do the opposite.

In basketball terms, this is managing minutes.

You do not overplay one lineup just because it scored early. Fatigue builds. Matchups change. What worked in the first quarter may not work late in the game. Smart coaches manage the rotation to stay effective for all four quarters.

Rebalancing enforces discipline when emotions would otherwise take over. It keeps risk aligned with intent instead of recent performance.

Rebalancing Is About Behavior, Not Prediction

Rebalancing is less about markets and more about behavior.

Left alone, portfolios drift.

Left unchecked, confidence grows.

Left unmanaged, risk increases.

Rebalancing acts as a guardrail. It prevents success from turning into overexposure and fear from turning into paralysis.

You are not reacting to headlines.

You are not guessing what happens next.

You are following a structure you already decided on.

That is professionalism.

Life Changes Matter as Much as Markets

Markets are not the only thing that change.

Life events matter just as much.

New job.

Marriage.

Children.

Buying a home.

Career transitions.

Each one alters timelines, responsibilities, and risk tolerance. Ignoring life changes while keeping the same portfolio is like running the same game plan against a completely different opponent.

Adjustments are not failure.

They are awareness.

What made sense earlier may no longer fit. That does not mean the original plan was wrong. It means circumstances evolved.

Your portfolio should evolve as your life evolves.

Avoiding Over-Coaching

Over-coaching ruins flow.

In basketball, too many instructions create hesitation. Players stop trusting instincts. Execution slows. Confidence drops.

The same thing happens with investing.

Constant tweaks increase costs, stress, and mistakes. Too much activity creates the illusion of control while quietly eroding results.

Discipline is not inactivity.

It is knowing when action is necessary and when it is not.

Sometimes the best adjustment is trusting what is already working. Letting a sound plan play out matters more than reacting to short-term noise.

A Coach's Perspective

A coach would remind you of a few core principles.

Make smart adjustments.

Do not overreact.

Trust the work you put in.

Let the game come to you.

Halftime is about clarity, not chaos.

Good coaches calm the room. They correct without panic. They keep the team focused on execution, not emotion. That mindset translates directly to financial decision-making.

Game Situations and Decision Points

These moments reveal discipline.

Markets move sharply. Do you rebalance according to plan, or do you panic and abandon structure?

Life changes. Do you update the portfolio, or do you ignore reality because change feels uncomfortable?

You feel restless. Do you act to feel productive, or do you stay disciplined and trust the process?

The right adjustment is often the calm one.

Athlete Habits and Financial Parallels

Athletes over-adjust.

Financially, that shows up as overtrading.

Athletes ignore feedback.

Financially, that leads to outdated portfolios.

Athletes confuse motion with improvement.

Financially, that creates noise and stress.

The same habits that disrupt flow on the court disrupt results with money.

Winning the Second Half

Rebalancing keeps you aligned.

Adjustments keep you relevant.

Discipline keeps you steady.

You do not win games by panicking at halftime. You win by making thoughtful changes and executing better in the second half.

That is where smart teams separate from emotional ones.

Athlete Takeaways

Review investments on a schedule, not constantly.

Rebalancing enforces discipline.

Life changes require portfolio updates.

Avoid over-coaching your investments.

Smart adjustments win long seasons.

The game is long.

Halftime is where composure matters most.

Chapter 18: The Mental Side of Money

The Mental Game: Why Emotion Determines Financial Outcomes

Every basketball player knows the game is not just physical. Talent matters. Conditioning matters. Skill matters. But the games that define seasons are usually decided mentally. Confidence. Composure. Focus. The ability to stay disciplined when the crowd gets loud and momentum swings.

Money works the same way.

Most financial mistakes are not caused by a lack of knowledge. They are caused by emotion. People often know what they should do. The challenge is executing it when conditions feel uncomfortable. Understanding the mental side of money is what separates disciplined decision-makers from reactive ones.

Fear, Greed, and Overconfidence

Three emotions drive most financial mistakes.

Fear shows up when markets drop.

Greed shows up when markets rise.

Overconfidence shows up when things are going well.

All three are dangerous.

Fear leads people to sell at the wrong time. Losses feel permanent even when they are not. Greed leads people to chase what is working right now, often after the easy gains are gone. Overconfidence leads people to ignore risk, assume skill where luck played a role, and abandon discipline.

In basketball terms, fear is hesitating on open shots. Greed is forcing contested ones. Overconfidence is ignoring the game plan because you feel unstoppable.

The emotions themselves are normal. Every athlete feels them. Every investor feels them. Acting on them without discipline is the mistake.

Mental toughness is not about eliminating emotion. It is about controlling behavior when emotion shows up.

Crowd Noise and Herd Behavior

Crowds influence games.

Momentum shifts. Fans get loud. Energy builds. Players feel pressure to respond. Sometimes that energy lifts performance. More often, it pulls players out of their role.

Financial markets have crowd noise too.

Headlines scream urgency. Social media amplifies extremes. Friends, coworkers, and commentators all have opinions when markets move. When prices rise, everyone feels smart. When prices fall, fear spreads quickly.

Herd behavior feels safe because you are not alone. If everyone is doing it, it must be right. In reality, herd behavior often leads to buying late and selling early.

In basketball terms, this is abandoning your assignment because the crowd reacts. You chase the ball instead of trusting the scheme. That usually leads to breakdowns.

Discipline means trusting your role, not reacting to noise.

Why Systems Matter More Than Willpower

Discipline is not about motivation.

Motivation fades. Emotion spikes. Willpower breaks down under stress. Systems are what keep execution consistent.

Strong financial systems include:

Automatic contributions.

Diversified portfolios.

Scheduled reviews.

Clear rules for when to act and when not to act.

These systems reduce decision-making during emotional moments. They protect you from yourself when pressure rises.

In basketball, players do not improvise under pressure without structure. They rely on plays, spacing, and defensive schemes. Those systems exist so players do not have to think their way through chaos.

Money works the same way.

If you rely on motivation, you will eventually make mistakes. If you rely on systems, you increase consistency.

Staying Focused During Market Swings

Market swings are unavoidable.

Prices rise. Prices fall. Volatility comes and goes. None of that means your plan is broken. What matters is how you respond.

Constantly checking balances increases anxiety. Every dip feels personal. Every surge feels like a signal. Changing strategies in the middle of a swing often locks in mistakes.

Staying focused means limiting noise, trusting the plan, and remembering why the strategy exists in the first place.

In basketball terms, this is staying locked in during a run by the other team. You slow the game down. You get a good shot. You trust fundamentals. You do not try to score ten points on one possession.

Focus is about controlling pace, not forcing action.

Confidence Versus Composure

Confidence matters, but composure matters more.

Confidence without structure becomes arrogance. Composure keeps you grounded when things are not going well and when things are going very well.

Many financial mistakes happen during success, not failure. When things are going well, people increase risk without realizing it. They abandon balance because recent results feel permanent.

In basketball, this is when teams stop running offense because shots are falling. Eventually, efficiency drops.

Composure means staying disciplined regardless of the score.

A Coach's Perspective

A coach would be direct.

Control what you can control.

Next play.

Stay composed.

Trust the process.

Coaches know mental toughness shows up when things get uncomfortable. Anyone can execute when everything is going well. The best players stay disciplined when things feel uncertain.

That is the difference between reacting and competing.

Game Situations and Decision Points

These moments reveal mindset.

Markets drop quickly. Do you react emotionally or stay disciplined?

Markets surge. Do you chase excitement or rebalance calmly?

Noise increases. Do you listen to the crowd or trust the plan?

The mental game determines outcomes long before the final score.

Athlete Habits and Financial Parallels

Athletes play to the crowd.

Financially, that shows up as herd behavior.

Athletes let emotion dictate decisions.

Financially, that leads to buying high and selling low.

Athletes ignore systems.

Financially, that results in inconsistency and stress.

The same habits that hurt performance on the court hurt results with money.

Winning the Long Game

The mental side of money is about discipline, focus, and emotional control.

Athletes who succeed financially treat money like competition. They prepare. They follow systems. They stay composed when pressure rises. They do not confuse emotion with insight.

Markets test patience.

Volatility tests discipline.

Noise tests focus.

Execution wins.

Athlete Takeaways

Fear, greed, and overconfidence distort decisions.

Crowd noise creates mistakes.

Systems beat willpower.

Focus matters most during volatility.

Stay composed and trust the plan.

The game is mental.

So is money.

Part V: The Long Season (Taxes, Family, and Life Stages)

B*asketball ends. Your financial decisions keep playing.*

Every basketball career ends.

Some end earlier than expected. Some end exactly on schedule. Very few end on your terms. What comes after is not a clean reset. It is a longer season with fewer whistles, less structure, and bigger consequences.

This is where money becomes real.

The long season is not about investing returns or market headlines. It is about decisions that shape your life year after year. Taxes. Housing. Careers. Family. Responsibilities that grow quietly but carry weight.

Athletes are conditioned to think in seasons. Preseason. Conference play. Postseason. Life does not work that way. Decisions overlap. Responsibilities stack. There is no offseason.

This part of the playbook focuses on long-term realities.

Taxes are not something you deal with once a year. They affect how much you keep, where you save, and how you invest. Housing decisions lock in obligations that last decades. Careers evolve. Income changes. Family dynamics introduce new priorities and boundaries.

None of these decisions feel dramatic in the moment.

They become powerful over time.

The mistake many former athletes make is treating these decisions as temporary. Assuming things will sort themselves out later. Later arrives faster than expected.

This section is about thinking beyond the next possession.

It is about understanding how life stages change the game plan. How responsibilities affect risk. How good decisions compound quietly while bad ones create pressure that is hard to escape.

Basketball taught you how to commit to a season.

This part teaches you how to commit to a life.

The long season rewards patience, planning, and discipline. It punishes avoidance and short-term thinking.

You may not hear the crowd anymore.

The scoreboard may not be visible.

But the game is still being played.

This section helps you stay prepared for it.

Chapter 19: Taxes and Where You Take Your Shots

Shot Selection: Why Taxes Decide How Much You Keep

Every basketball player understands shot selection.

An open layup.

A rhythm three.

A contested fadeaway early in the clock.

All shots count the same on the scoreboard, but they do not carry the same probability. Smart players know where their best shots come from, how to create them, and when to pass instead of forcing something difficult.

Taxes work the same way.

It is not just about how much you earn. It is about how much you keep. Where you take your financial shots matters just as much as the shots themselves. Two investors can earn the same return and end up with very different results based solely on tax efficiency.

This chapter is about choosing better shots, not taking more of them.

Taxable and Tax-Advantaged Accounts

There are two broad categories where investments live.

Taxable accounts and tax-advantaged accounts.

Taxable accounts offer flexibility. You can invest, rebalance, and access money at any time. The tradeoff is taxes along the way. Dividends, interest, and realized gains are typically taxed as they occur.

Tax-advantaged accounts are designed for long-term planning. Retirement accounts, health savings accounts, and similar vehicles allow growth to be taxed differently. Some delay taxes. Some eliminate them entirely if rules are followed.

In basketball terms, taxable accounts are pull-up jumpers.

They are available anytime.

They are useful in many situations.

They are less efficient over time.

Tax-advantaged accounts are shots at the rim.

Harder to access.

More rules.

Higher efficiency.

The mistake is treating one as good and the other as bad. Smart players use both. Balance matters.

Tax-Deferred and Tax-Free Growth

Within tax-advantaged accounts, there are two main structures.

Tax-deferred growth and tax-free growth.

Tax-deferred growth means you delay taxes until later. Contributions may reduce taxes today, but withdrawals are taxed in the future. The benefit is compounding without annual tax drag.

Tax-free growth means you pay taxes now and withdraw later without tax, assuming rules are met. The benefit is certainty. What you see is what you keep.

Neither is automatically better.

The right choice depends on current income, future income expectations, career trajectory, and timing. Making the wrong assumption about the future can create regret. Making no decision at all usually does too.

In basketball terms, this is choosing between two-point shots and three-point shots.

Both score.

Both have tradeoffs.

Context determines which is better.

The mistake is letting convenience dictate decisions instead of understanding the situation.

Asset Location: Using the Floor Properly

Asset allocation determines what you own.

Asset location determines where you hold it.

This distinction matters.

Some investments generate regular taxable income. Others are more tax-efficient by nature. Holding them in the wrong account increases tax drag without increasing return.

Asset location is about placing investments in the most appropriate accounts to improve after-tax results.

In basketball terms, this is spacing.

You do not clog the paint with shooters.

You do not leave the perimeter empty.

You place players where they are most effective.

Good spacing improves efficiency without requiring more effort. Asset location works the same way. You are not changing what you own. You are improving how it performs after taxes.

This is one of the most overlooked areas of investing because it is not exciting. It does not feel like a big move. Over time, it makes a meaningful difference.

Why Taxes Deserve Ongoing Attention

Many people treat taxes as a once-a-year problem.

They scramble at filing time.

They react to headlines.

They make decisions late.

Taxes reward planning, not reaction.

Good tax decisions are made throughout the year. They are built into saving, investing, and withdrawal strategies. Waiting until the last minute limits options and increases stress.

In basketball terms, this is preparing in practice instead of improvising in the fourth quarter. Late adjustments are harder. Early positioning makes execution easier.

Common Tax Mistakes

The same mistakes show up again and again.

Ignoring taxes entirely and focusing only on returns.

Using only one type of account because it feels simpler.

Making decisions based on tax headlines instead of personal context.

Waiting until filing season to think about strategy.

These mistakes are not caused by lack of intelligence. They are caused by lack of structure. Taxes do not need to dominate decisions, but they cannot be ignored.

Efficiency matters.

A Coach's Perspective

A coach would emphasize fundamentals.

Take good shots.

Use the floor properly.

Do not waste possessions.

Taxes are part of the game whether you like it or not. Ignoring them does not make them disappear. It just lowers efficiency over time.

Smart teams do not need to be perfect. They need to be intentional.

Game Situations and Decision Points

These moments shape outcomes.

You earn more. Do you adjust where you save, or do you keep shooting from the same spot?

You invest. Do you consider tax impact, or do you ignore it because it feels complicated?

You reach late in the year. Do you plan ahead, or do you scramble?

Good shot selection shows up before the ball leaves your hands.

Athlete Habits and Financial Parallels

Athletes force shots.

Financially, that means ignoring taxes.

Athletes ignore spacing.

Financially, that means poor asset location.

Athletes react late.

Financially, that leads to missed opportunities.

The same habits that lower efficiency on the court lower results with money.

Winning Through Efficiency

You cannot avoid taxes.

You can manage them.

Choosing where to take your shots improves efficiency without increasing risk. Over time, small improvements compound into meaningful advantages.

You do not need trick plays.

You need better shot selection.

Athlete Takeaways

Where you invest matters as much as what you invest.

Tax-advantaged accounts improve efficiency.

Tax-deferred and tax-free growth serve different roles.

Asset location improves spacing.

Smart shot selection keeps more points on the board.

Efficiency wins games.

It also builds wealth.

Chapter 20: Retirement Accounts and Financial Independence

Playing for the Fourth Quarter: How Retirement Planning Creates Freedom

Every athlete understands preparation for a future moment.

You train in the offseason for games you have not played yet. You lift for strength you will need later. You watch film to avoid mistakes before they happen. None of that work shows up immediately, but when the moment arrives, you are ready.

Preparation creates freedom.

Retirement planning works the same way.

Financial independence is not about a specific age. It is about options. It is the ability to make decisions without being forced by money. Retirement accounts are tools designed to help you build those options over time, quietly and consistently.

They are not exciting.

They are effective.

Employer Plans: Using What Is Already There

For many people, an employer retirement plan is the first opportunity to invest consistently.

401(k)s and similar plans allow you to save directly from your paycheck. Contributions happen automatically. You do not have to remember to invest. Discipline is built into the system.

Many employers also offer matching contributions. That match is not a bonus. It is part of your compensation.

In basketball terms, an employer match is a fast-break opportunity. You do not jog back on defense when the lane is open. You take the easy points.

Ignoring an employer match is leaving value on the table. Even modest contributions add up over time when paired with consistency and compounding.

The goal is not perfection.

The goal is participation.

Automatic Contributions Build Consistency

One of the most powerful features of employer plans is automation.

Money is invested before you see it. That reduces friction. It removes emotion. It turns saving into a habit instead of a decision.

Athletes understand this. You do not wait to feel motivated to train. You follow the program. Over time, the work accumulates.

Small contributions made consistently often outperform larger contributions made sporadically. Consistency matters more than timing.

Traditional and Roth IRAs: Expanding Your Options

Individual Retirement Accounts give you flexibility beyond employer plans.

Traditional IRAs offer tax-deferred growth. You may receive a tax benefit now, and taxes are paid later when money is withdrawn.

Roth IRAs offer tax-free growth. You pay taxes now, and qualified withdrawals later are not taxed.

Neither is automatically better.

The right choice depends on income, career trajectory, tax expectations, and long-term goals. For some, tax savings today matter most. For others, tax certainty later is more valuable.

In basketball terms, these are different scoring options.

Both count.

Both have tradeoffs.

Context determines which is best.

Using both types can create balance and flexibility down the road.

Rules Are Part of the Design

Retirement accounts come with rules.

Contribution limits.

Withdrawal restrictions.

Penalties for early access.

These rules exist for a reason. They are not punishments. They are structure designed to encourage long-term behavior.

In basketball terms, this is the shot clock.

The shot clock creates urgency, but it also creates flow. It prevents stagnation. It forces discipline. Without structure, the game falls apart.

Understanding the rules helps you avoid unnecessary fouls. It allows you to plan ahead instead of reacting later. Knowing what you can and cannot do matters as much as knowing where you want to go.

Retirement Is Not a Single Moment

Many people think of retirement as a finish line.

In reality, it is a phase.

Saving for retirement is one challenge. Using retirement savings effectively is another. Retirement income planning focuses on how money is withdrawn, how taxes are managed, and how long assets need to last.

This is where preparation pays off.

In basketball terms, this is late-game execution. You do not change your identity in the final minutes. You rely on fundamentals. You manage the clock. You protect the lead.

The goal is sustainability, not maximum withdrawals. Running out of money late in life is the equivalent of blowing a lead because you rushed the offense.

Time Is the Biggest Advantage

Retirement planning rewards time more than anything else.

Starting earlier gives compounding more opportunities to work. Delaying means you have to work harder later for the same result.

This is not about regret. It is about awareness.

You do not need to start big.

You do need to start.

Even small contributions made early can create meaningful outcomes over long periods. Preparation does not require perfection. It requires commitment.

A Coach's Perspective

A coach would emphasize patience and discipline.

Trust the process.

Take advantage of opportunities.

Think long term.

Protect future options.

Coaches know championships are not won in one practice or one game. They are built through consistency, repetition, and preparation long before the spotlight arrives.

Retirement planning works the same way.

Game Situations and Decision Points

These moments shape outcomes.

Your employer offers a match. Do you take it, or do you tell yourself you will start later?

You qualify for an IRA. Do you use it, or do you delay because it feels complicated?

You want flexibility in the future. Do you prepare now, or do you hope it works out later?

Preparation creates options. Options create freedom.

Athlete Habits and Financial Parallels

Athletes skip offseason work.

Financially, that shows up as delaying retirement savings.

Athletes focus only on scoring.

Financially, that means ignoring income planning.

Athletes underestimate longevity.

Financially, that leads to running out of money.

The habits that shorten careers on the court shorten financial independence off it.

Winning the Long Game

Financial independence is built slowly and deliberately.

Retirement accounts are not exciting. They are powerful. They reward consistency, patience, and respect for structure.

Use them consistently.

Understand the rules.

Let time do the work.

Preparation today creates freedom later.

Athlete Takeaways

Retirement accounts create future options.

Employer matches are free points.

Traditional and Roth accounts play different roles.

Rules create discipline, not restriction.

Consistent preparation leads to independence.

You do not train for today's game alone.

You train for the future you want.

Chapter 21: Housing and Big Financial Decisions

Slow the Game Down: Making Big Financial Decisions Without Forcing It

Big financial decisions feel like major moments.

Buying a home. Financing a car. Signing a long lease. Making a purchase that commits you to years of payments. These decisions do not happen every month, but when they do, they shape everything that follows.

Basketball players understand this instinctively.

You do not rush big moments. You slow the game down. You check the clock. You understand the score, the matchup, and the situation. Big decisions require awareness, not emotion.

Money works the same way.

Renting and Buying Are Tools, Not Identities

Renting and buying are often treated like personal labels instead of financial tools. That framing causes mistakes.

Renting offers flexibility.

Lower upfront costs.

Easier exits.

Fewer long-term commitments.

It is often the right move early in a career, during relocations, or when income or location is uncertain.

Buying offers stability.

Potential appreciation.

Forced savings through mortgage payments.

Control over your space.

It can make sense when income is steady, timelines are long, and flexibility matters less.

In basketball terms, renting is staying light on your feet. You can change direction quickly. Buying is posting up and establishing position. You absorb contact, but mobility decreases.

Neither option is better in every situation.

The mistake is buying because it feels like progress or adulthood rather than because it fits your actual life. Progress that reduces flexibility too early often becomes pressure.

Mortgages Are Bigger Than the Payment

A mortgage is long-term debt tied to a physical asset.

The monthly payment matters.

The interest rate matters.

The loan length matters.

But those are not the only factors.

Owning a home also brings responsibility.

Maintenance.

Property taxes.

Insurance.

Unexpected repairs.

Time and attention.

In basketball terms, this is committing to heavy minutes.

Heavy minutes require conditioning.

They require recovery.

They require depth.

If income is unstable, job mobility matters, or flexibility is important, heavy minutes can hurt you late in the game.

Down payments play a role here.

A larger down payment can reduce monthly pressure and interest costs.

A smaller down payment preserves cash and flexibility.

There is no universal rule. The right choice depends on cash reserves, income stability, and future plans. Anyone giving one-size-fits-all advice is ignoring context.

Cars, Leases, and Financing Traps

Cars are one of the most common financial traps.

They depreciate.

They feel necessary.

They are easy to finance.

They are marketed emotionally.

Monthly payments often look manageable in isolation. The problem shows up when those payments stack with housing, insurance, savings goals, and everyday expenses.

Leases can offer lower monthly payments, but they limit flexibility and lock you into rules. Long loans can reduce monthly costs, but they increase total cost and keep you upside down longer.

In basketball terms, this is taking a flashy shot that looks good but hurts efficiency.

Cars should support your life.

They should get you where you need to go.

They should not become a scoreboard or status symbol.

Transportation is a tool, not a reward.

Planning Big Purchases the Right Way

Big purchases deserve planning, not impulse.

That means understanding the full cost, not just the monthly payment. It means knowing how the purchase affects cash flow, savings, and flexibility.

Ask better questions.

Can you still build emergency savings?

Can you still contribute to retirement?

Can you absorb a surprise expense?

Can you sleep at night with the commitment?

If one purchase forces you to sacrifice all margin, it is too big.

In basketball terms, this is shot selection late in the game. You do not take a difficult look if it compromises everything else. You protect the possession.

Qualification Is Not the Same as Readiness

One of the most dangerous phrases in personal finance is, "You qualify."

Qualifying for a loan does not mean you should take it.

Affording a payment does not mean it fits your life.

Approval is not advice.

Lenders measure risk differently than you should. Their goal is repayment. Your goal is sustainability.

In basketball terms, just because you can take a shot does not mean you should. Awareness matters more than capability.

A Coach's Perspective

A coach would slow you down.

Know the situation.

Check the clock.

Make the simple play.

Do not force it.

Big decisions deserve patience. Rushed choices create long recoveries.

Calm decisions preserve options.

Great players do not panic in big moments. They rely on fundamentals.

Game Situations and Decision Points

These moments reveal discipline.

You feel pressure to buy. Do you evaluate fit, or do you chase status?

You qualify for financing. Do you ask whether you should take it, or just whether you can?

You want something now. Do you consider the long-term impact, or only the immediate feeling?

The moment passes.

The decision lasts.

Athlete Habits and Financial Parallels

Athletes rush big moments.

Financially, that leads to overcommitment.

Athletes focus on highlights.

Financially, that leads to expensive purchases.

Athletes underestimate recovery time.

Financially, that leads to stress and regret.

The same habits that create turnovers late in games create pressure in life.

Winning With Margin

Housing and large purchases should support your life, not restrict it.

Flexibility matters.

Cash flow matters.

Peace of mind matters.

The smartest decision is often the one that keeps options open. You do not win long seasons by exhausting yourself early.

You win by managing energy, resources, and commitment.

Athlete Takeaways

Renting and buying serve different seasons of life.

Mortgages require stability and planning.

Cars should be tools, not trophies.

Monthly payments hide long-term costs.

Big decisions deserve patience and clarity.

Slow the game down.

Good decisions come from awareness, not pressure.

Chapter 22: Your Career Is Your Franchise Player

Develop Your Franchise Player: Why Your Career Drives Everything Else

Every team is built around a franchise player.

Not just the most talented one, but the one everything else depends on. Lineups adjust around them. The system is designed to maximize their strengths. When they are healthy, improving, and supported, the entire organization benefits. When they stagnate or struggle, everything else feels harder.

Your career plays that same role in your financial life.

Investments matter. Budgets matter. Protection matters. But nothing drives your financial outcomes more than your ability to earn, grow, and adapt over time. Treating your career casually is like ignoring the development of your best player and hoping the rest of the roster carries the load.

It rarely works.

Salary Is Not the Full Picture

Most people evaluate jobs by salary alone.

That is understandable. Salary is visible. It is easy to compare. It feels concrete. But salary is only one part of total compensation, and often not the most important one.

Total compensation includes bonuses, retirement contributions, health insurance, time off, flexibility, career development, and long-term opportunity. Two roles with the same salary can produce very different financial outcomes depending on what comes with them.

In basketball terms, salary is points per game.

Total compensation is efficiency, defense, minutes, role, and impact. You would never evaluate a player using only one stat. Doing so with your career leads to bad decisions.

Understanding total compensation helps you avoid chasing headlines and instead focus on fit and sustainability.

Job Changes Reset the System

Changing jobs is like changing teams.

New offense.

New expectations.

New culture.

New benefits.

Every move resets certain variables. Health insurance changes. Retirement plans reset. Vesting schedules restart. Paid time off and flexibility shift. These details affect cash flow, stress, and long-term planning more than most people expect.

In basketball terms, this is learning a new playbook. You cannot judge the system before you understand it. Jumping teams without evaluating the full structure can create instability that spills into every financial decision.

Job changes can accelerate growth when planned well. Poorly timed moves create friction that shows up as stress, rushed decisions, and lost momentum.

Movement is not progress by default. Intentional movement is.

Negotiation Is a Skill, Not a Confrontation

Many people avoid negotiating because it feels uncomfortable.

Athletes know this feeling. You have competed for minutes, roles, and opportunities your entire life. Negotiation uses the same skills. Preparation. Awareness. Confidence. Timing.

Negotiation is not confrontation. It is communication.

In basketball terms, negotiation is positioning. You do not demand the ball without earning trust. You demonstrate value, understand leverage, and communicate clearly. The same applies to compensation discussions.

Small improvements compound.

A slightly higher salary.

A better retirement match.

More flexibility.

Clearer growth paths.

These changes may feel minor in the moment, but over a career they add up to meaningful differences. Avoiding negotiation out of discomfort is leaving value on the table.

Side Income and Expanding Your Game

Side income can increase flexibility.

Coaching.

Consulting.

Content creation.

Business ownership.

Freelance work.

These opportunities can supplement income, build skills, and create optionality. They can also introduce complexity, taxes, and risk if not managed intentionally.

In basketball terms, this is expanding your game.

Adding a reliable midrange shot makes you harder to guard. Taking every shot without structure creates chaos. Side income should complement your main role, not compete with it.

The mistake is chasing side income for excitement or comparison rather than purpose. Side income works best when it supports your primary career and long-term goals.

Protecting the Asset That Funds Everything

Your career funds every other part of your financial plan.

It pays for investments.

It supports savings.

It enables flexibility.

It absorbs setbacks.

Ignoring career development while obsessing over investment details is misaligned effort. You cannot out-invest a stalled income forever. Skill development, reputation, and adaptability matter.

Just like a franchise player, your career requires maintenance.

Training.

Learning.

Recovery.

Adjustment.

Burnout is the equivalent of injury. Overextension without support shortens careers. Sustainable progress beats short bursts of effort.

A Coach's Perspective

A coach would be direct.

Develop your best player.

Know your value.

Play within the system.

Think long term.

Great organizations invest in their franchise player because everything else flows from that foundation. Your career deserves the same attention.

Game Situations and Decision Points

These moments shape trajectories.

You receive a job offer. Do you evaluate total compensation or focus only on salary?

You feel underpaid. Do you prepare and negotiate, or stay silent and hope things change?

You want side income. Do you plan for impact and risk, or chase quick money without structure?

Career decisions echo for years. They deserve deliberate thought.

Athlete Habits and Financial Parallels

Athletes rely on talent alone.

Financially, that means neglecting development.

Athletes avoid uncomfortable conversations.

Financially, that means leaving money and opportunity on the table.

Athletes overextend.

Financially, that leads to burnout and instability.

The habits that shorten careers on the court shorten earning potential off it.

Winning the Long Game

Careers are built, not discovered.

They are shaped through skill development, intentional decisions, and awareness of trade-offs. When your franchise player is healthy, growing, and supported, every other financial decision becomes easier.

Invest in skills.

Protect flexibility.

Make intentional moves.

Everything else works better when the foundation is strong.

Athlete Takeaways

Your career drives every financial outcome.

Total compensation matters more than salary alone.

Job changes reset benefits, risks, and momentum.

Negotiation rewards preparation and confidence.

Side income should support, not distract from, your main game.

Develop your franchise player.

The rest of the system depends on it.

Chapter 23: Estate Planning Basics Everyone Needs

Calling the Play in Advance: Why Estate Planning Is About Control

Estate planning sounds like something far off.

Something for older people.

Something you will deal with later.

Something that does not apply yet.

That mindset causes more damage than almost any other financial delay.

Estate planning is not about death. It is about control. It is about making sure decisions are made by the right people, at the right time, without confusion, conflict, or unnecessary cost.

Basketball players understand this instinctively.

You do not wait until the final seconds to decide who takes the last shot. You define roles ahead of time. You know who handles the ball, who spaces the floor, and who is trusted when pressure hits. Estate planning does the same thing for life.

It removes guesswork when stakes are high.

Wills: The Basic Game Plan

A will is a set of instructions.

It outlines who receives your assets, who is responsible for handling your affairs, and who makes decisions for minor children if applicable. It provides direction when you are no longer able to give it yourself.

Without a will, the state decides.

That process is slow.

It is expensive.

It is impersonal.

Courts do not know your priorities. They follow rules, not intentions. The result is often delays, added costs, and outcomes you would not have chosen.

In basketball terms, a will is a basic game plan.

It is not complicated.

It is not flashy.

It gives structure instead of chaos.

A basic plan executed is always better than no plan at all.

Trusts: Installing the Full System

A trust is a more advanced planning tool.

It can provide privacy, efficiency, and control over how and when assets are distributed. Trusts can help manage assets during incapacity, reduce delays, and create clearer outcomes for those you care about.

Trusts are not only for wealthy families.

They are for people who want clarity.

They are for people who want structure.

They are for people who want fewer problems left behind.

In basketball terms, a trust is a fully installed system.

The reads are clear.

The responsibilities are defined.

Execution is smoother under pressure.

Not everyone needs the same system, but everyone benefits from having one.

Beneficiaries and Account Titling Matter More Than You Think

Many assets do not pass through a will.

Retirement accounts.

Insurance policies.

Bank and investment accounts.

These assets transfer based on beneficiary designations. If those forms are outdated or incorrect, your intentions may not matter at all.

Account titling matters too.

How assets are owned affects taxes, access, and control. Joint ownership, individual ownership, and trust ownership all come with different outcomes.

In basketball terms, this is lineup clarity.

If roles are unclear, confusion shows up when it matters most. Missed assignments lead to breakdowns. In estate planning, unclear beneficiaries lead to delays, disputes, and unnecessary costs.

These mistakes are common.

They are preventable.

They are expensive.

Powers of Attorney: Planning for Incapacity

A power of attorney allows someone to act on your behalf if you cannot.

A financial power of attorney covers money decisions. A healthcare power of attorney covers medical decisions. These documents are critical during illness, injury, or temporary incapacity.

Without them, loved ones may be unable to help you even if they want to. Bills go unpaid. Decisions get delayed. Stress increases at exactly the wrong time.

In basketball terms, this is having a backup point guard.

If you are unavailable, the game still needs to be run. You do not leave the team without leadership when pressure hits.

Planning for incapacity is not pessimism. It is realism.

Healthcare Directives Remove Guesswork

Healthcare directives outline your medical wishes.

They guide doctors.

They guide loved ones.

They remove uncertainty during serious situations.

These conversations are uncomfortable. Avoiding them does not protect anyone. It simply transfers stress and responsibility to others when emotions are already high.

In basketball terms, this is film review for tough situations.

You prepare in advance so teammates are not guessing in real time. Clear instructions reduce mistakes and conflict.

Preparation is an act of care.

Estate Planning Evolves With Life

Estate planning is not a one-time event.

Life changes.

Relationships change.

Assets change.

Responsibilities change.

Marriage, children, divorce, new assets, or major moves all require updates. Ignoring changes creates misalignment between intent and reality.

In basketball terms, this is refusing to adjust the game plan when the opponent changes strategy. What worked before may no longer fit.

Updating documents is not a sign something is wrong. It is a sign you are paying attention.

A Coach's Perspective

A coach would be blunt.

Handle your business.

Do not leave decisions to chance.

Protect the team.

Prepare for what you cannot control.

Good teams plan for pressure before it arrives. Estate planning does the same thing.

Responsibility is not fear.

It is leadership.

Game Situations and Decision Points

These moments define outcomes.

You assume you are too young. Do you delay or take control?

Your life changes. Do you update documents or ignore them?

You want simplicity. Do you create clarity now or confusion later?

Preparation always matters more than timing.

Athlete Habits and Financial Parallels

Athletes avoid uncomfortable planning.

Financially, that leads to chaos.

Athletes assume someone else will handle it.

Financially, that leads to delays and conflict.

Athletes wait too long.

Financially, that increases cost and stress.

The same habits that hurt teams late hurt families later.

Winning the Long Game

Estate planning is not about predicting the future.

It is about removing uncertainty.

Clear instructions.

The right people.

The right timing.

That is how professionals protect what they build and the people they care about.

Athlete Takeaways

Estate planning is about control, not age.

Wills and trusts create clarity and structure.

Beneficiary designations matter more than people realize.

Powers of attorney protect you when you cannot act.

Preparation removes pressure from the people you care about.

You would not wait until the last possession to decide the play.

Do not wait to decide this one either.

Chapter 24: Talking About Money With Family and Teammates

Money conversations are uncomfortable.

Not because money is complicated, but because it is emotional. Expectations, guilt, pride, history, and fear all show up at once. Many people avoid these conversations until circumstances force them. By then, the stakes are higher and the options are fewer.

Athletes understand this dynamic.

Teams that communicate clearly handle pressure better. Teams that avoid hard conversations break down when adversity hits. Money works the same way.

This chapter is about communication, boundaries, and leadership, not control.

Teaching Kids About Money

Kids learn money the same way they learn basketball.

By watching.

By repetition.

By habits, not lectures.

Teaching kids about money does not require advanced lessons. It requires consistency and age-appropriate responsibility. Saving a portion of what they receive. Making spending choices. Waiting for something they want.

In basketball terms, this is fundamentals camp. You are not installing complex sets. You are teaching footwork and spacing. What kids learn early becomes normal later.

College and Young Adults

This is where financial habits accelerate.

First paychecks. Credit cards. Student loans. Independence. Consequences arrive faster than expected.

Young adults need guidance without control. Clear expectations. Real consequences. Support paired with accountability.

In basketball terms, this is the jump from high school to college ball. The speed increases. Mistakes are exposed faster. Coaching still matters, but ownership increases.

Avoid rescuing every mistake. Teach decision-making.

Aging Parents and Caregiving

Eventually, roles shift.

Parents age. Health changes. Financial responsibilities increase. These conversations are emotional and often delayed, but delay creates stress and confusion.

Addressing these topics early allows for planning, shared responsibility, and clarity. Ignoring them forces decisions during crisis.

In basketball terms, this is leadership in the fourth quarter. You step up because the team needs it, not because it is comfortable.

Family Expectations and Boundaries

This is where many former athletes struggle the most.

Success creates expectations. Income creates assumptions. Family and friends may see you as a solution rather than a person with limits.

Helping without boundaries leads to resentment, instability, and burnout. Boundaries are not selfish. They are protective.

In basketball terms, this is understanding your role. You cannot guard everyone and score every possession. You have to play within a system.

Support should be intentional, planned, and sustainable. Emotional decisions feel generous in the moment and damaging over time.

Coach's Perspective

A coach would be direct.

Communicate early.

Set expectations.

Protect the team.

Do not avoid hard conversations.

Leadership off the court matters just as much.

Game Situations and Decision Points

A family member needs help. Do you respond emotionally or intentionally?

A young adult struggles. Do you guide or enable?

Expectations increase as income grows. Do you set boundaries or hope it works out?

The conversation changes the outcome.

Common Athlete Mistakes and Financial Parallels

Athletes avoid conflict.

Financially, that leads to misunderstanding.

Athletes try to carry everything alone.

Financially, that leads to burnout.

Athletes confuse loyalty with obligation.

Financially, that leads to instability.

Winning the Long Game

Money conversations do not get easier by avoiding them.

They get easier by being clear, honest, and proactive. Communication protects relationships. Boundaries protect progress.

Both are necessary.

Athlete Takeaways

- Money conversations are leadership moments.
- Teach kids through habits, not lectures.
- Young adults need guidance and accountability.
- Aging parents require planning and empathy.
- Boundaries protect both relationships and financial stability.

Chapter 24: Talking About Money With Family and Teammates ● Teaching kids about money ● College and young adults ● Aging parents and caregiving ● Family expectations and boundaries

Chapter 24: Talking About Money With Family and Teammates

Money conversations are some of the hardest conversations to have.

Not because the numbers are complicated, but because money is tied to emotion, history, pride, guilt, and expectation. Many people avoid these discussions until a problem forces them. By then, the pressure is high and the options are limited.

Athletes recognize this pattern.

Teams that communicate clearly handle adversity better. Teams that avoid hard conversations break down when stress shows up. Money works the same way. Silence creates confusion. Clarity creates stability.

This chapter is about leadership, communication, and boundaries.

Teaching Kids About Money

Kids learn money the same way they learn sports.

They watch first.

They copy habits.

They repeat what feels normal.

You do not need complex lessons or spreadsheets. You need consistency. Simple rules. Clear expectations.

Saving part of what they receive.

Spending with intention.

Waiting for things they want.

In basketball terms, this is fundamentals training. You are not teaching advanced sets. You are teaching footwork and balance. What kids experience early becomes instinct later.

College and Young Adults

This stage is where money decisions speed up.

First paychecks. Credit cards. Student loans. Freedom. Mistakes can happen quickly and compound quietly.

Young adults need guidance without control. They need information, boundaries, and consequences. Not rescue. Not silence.

In basketball terms, this is the transition from practice to real minutes. The game is faster. The margin for error is smaller. Coaching still matters, but ownership increases.

Helping means teaching decision-making, not eliminating discomfort.

Aging Parents and Caregiving

Eventually, roles shift.

Parents age. Health changes. Financial responsibilities increase. These conversations are emotional and uncomfortable, which is why they are often delayed.

Delay creates confusion. Planning creates clarity.

Talking about finances, healthcare wishes, and responsibilities early reduces stress later. It allows families to share the load instead of reacting in crisis.

In basketball terms, this is leadership in late-game situations. You step up because the team needs it.

Family Expectations and Boundaries

This is where many former athletes struggle the most.

Success changes how people see you. Income creates assumptions. Family and friends may view you as a solution instead of a person with limits.

Helping without boundaries leads to resentment, instability, and burnout. Boundaries are not selfish. They are necessary.

In basketball terms, you cannot guard everyone and take every shot. You have a role. Playing outside it hurts the team.

Support should be intentional, planned, and sustainable. Emotional decisions feel generous in the moment and damaging over time.

Coach's Perspective

A coach would be direct.

Communicate early.

Set expectations.

Protect the team.

Do not avoid uncomfortable conversations.

Leadership off the court matters too.

Game Situations and Decision Points

A family member asks for help. Do you respond emotionally or with a plan?

A young adult struggles financially. Do you guide or enable?

Expectations rise as income grows. Do you set boundaries or hope it works out?

The conversation changes the outcome.

Common Athlete Mistakes and Financial Parallels

Athletes avoid conflict.

Financially, that leads to misunderstanding.

Athletes try to carry everything alone.

Financially, that leads to burnout.

Athletes confuse loyalty with obligation.

Financially, that leads to instability.

Winning the Long Game

Money conversations do not get easier by avoiding them.

They get easier through honesty, clarity, and consistency. Communication protects relationships. Boundaries protect progress.

Both are required to win long term.

Athlete Takeaways

- Money conversations are leadership moments.
- Teach kids through habits, not lectures.
- Young adults need guidance and accountability.
- Aging parents require planning and empathy.
- Clear boundaries protect relationships and financial stability.

Part VI: Winning Beyond the Scoreboard

The scoreboard eventually goes dark.

The crowd leaves. The lights shut off. The uniform gets hung up for the last time. What remains is not your stat line or your highlight reel. What remains is the life you built once the game stopped keeping score for you.

This is the part most athletes are not prepared for.

Sports provide structure. Clear rules. Clear feedback. Clear winners and losers. Life after sports removes those guardrails. Success becomes quieter. Progress becomes harder to measure. Comparison becomes dangerous.

Winning beyond the scoreboard means redefining what success actually looks like.

This final part of the playbook focuses on long-term decision-making, character, and perspective. It is about protecting what you have built and recognizing traps that do not show up on a box score. It is about knowing when to ask for help, how to avoid bad advice, and how to keep moving forward without chasing validation.

Money is still involved, but it is no longer the point.

The point is alignment.

Alignment between your values and your decisions. Between your time and your priorities. Between who you were as an athlete and who you are becoming as a person.

Many former athletes struggle here because they keep chasing the feeling of competition instead of building a sustainable version of purpose. Winning beyond the scoreboard means finding fulfillment without needing a crowd.

It means building systems that support your health, your family, your community, and your future. It means recognizing that some of the most important wins do not feel dramatic in the moment.

No buzzer sounds to end this game.

You keep playing.

This section helps you do it with clarity, confidence, and intention.

Chapter 25: Advisors, Scams, and Playing the Long Game

Building the Right Team: When Help Becomes a Competitive Advantage

Every athlete eventually needs help.

Not because they are weak, but because the game gets bigger. More complex. Harder to manage alone. As competition rises, no player succeeds without support. Coaches. Trainers. Medical staff. Film analysts. Each plays a role in keeping performance high over long seasons.

Money works the same way.

At some point, the right move is not doing more yourself. It is building the right team around you. This chapter is about knowing who belongs in your circle, what role they should play, and how to avoid people who do not deserve a seat on the bench.

Knowing When to Seek Professional Help

You do not wait until you are injured to meet the trainer.

You build relationships early so support is already in place when pressure rises. Financial help works the same way. Professional guidance becomes valuable when decisions affect taxes, investments, insurance, family planning, or long-term outcomes.

Complexity is a signal, not a failure.

As income grows, responsibilities expand, and life becomes more layered, the margin for error shrinks. Trying to manage everything alone often leads to missed opportunities or preventable mistakes.

Seeking help is not weakness. It is leverage.

In basketball terms, this is trusting the coaching staff. Talent alone is not enough. Preparation, structure, and perspective matter just as much.

Understanding the Different Roles Advisors Play

Not all financial advisors play the same role.

Some focus primarily on investments.

Some focus on planning and coordination.

Some sell specific products.

Some act as quarterbacks who oversee everything.

Understanding what an advisor does, and how they are compensated, matters more than titles. Incentives drive behavior. Alignment matters.

In basketball terms, this is knowing positions.

You do not expect a center to run the offense.

You do not expect a point guard to protect the rim.

You do not expect one role to cover everything.

Clarity prevents disappointment. When expectations match reality, the relationship works. When they do not, frustration follows.

Before trusting someone with major decisions, understand their role, their responsibility, and how they get paid.

Recognizing Scams and Bad Advice

Scams do not target intelligence.

They target emotion.

Urgency.

Exclusivity.

Guarantees.

Pressure to act quickly.

Promises of certainty.

If something sounds too good to be true, it usually is. Legitimate strategies do not require secrecy or speed. Real planning allows time for questions, reflection, and verification.

In basketball terms, this is biting on every pump fake.

Defenders who jump at everything get beaten. Discipline protects you. So does patience.

Anyone pushing you to rush a decision, avoid outside opinions, or ignore risk is not on your team.

Ten Common Financial Mistakes That Quietly Compound

Mistakes rarely show up all at once. They build slowly.

Chasing quick wins instead of sustainable progress.

Ignoring taxes until it is too late.

Overspending early when income rises.

Delaying saving and investing.

Taking on too much concentrated risk.

Avoiding uncomfortable planning conversations.

Trusting the wrong people.

Letting emotion dictate decisions.

Failing to set boundaries with money and time.

Doing nothing out of fear of doing something wrong.

None of these mistakes feel catastrophic in the moment. Over time, they compound into stress, regret, and lost opportunity.

Awareness prevents most of them.

Ten Rules That Actually Work Over the Long Run

There is no secret system.

There are principles.

Live below your means.

Save consistently.

Invest with discipline.

Diversify risk.

Manage taxes intentionally.

Protect yourself with appropriate insurance.

Keep systems simple.

Communicate clearly with people involved in your finances.

Adjust as life changes.

Stay patient and committed.

These rules are boring.

They work.

Championship teams do not rely on trick plays every possession. They rely on fundamentals executed well.

Why Simplicity Is a Competitive Advantage

Many people confuse complexity with sophistication.

In reality, complexity increases mistakes. More accounts. More products. More decisions. More stress.

Simple systems are easier to maintain under pressure. They allow you to focus on execution instead of constant management.

In basketball terms, this is running offense instead of improvising every possession. Structure creates freedom.

A Coach's Perspective

A coach would keep it straightforward.

Build the right team.

Do not chase shortcuts.

Trust the process.

Play for the long season.

Great coaches know talent needs structure. The same is true financially.

Playing the Long Game

The long game is not exciting.

It is consistent.

Disciplined.

Intentional.

Wins do not come from one big play. They come from thousands of small, smart decisions stacked over time. Most success stories look boring from the outside. That is not a flaw. It is the point.

You do not need to be perfect.

You need to stay in the game.

That requires support, clarity, and alignment.

Athlete Takeaways

Asking for help is a strength, not a weakness.

Know who is on your team and why.

Scams prey on urgency and emotion.

Small mistakes compound into big problems.

Long-term success comes from discipline, patience, and alignment.

No athlete wins alone.

Money is no different.

Chapter 26: Losing the Schedule and Rebuilding Structure

When the Whistle Stops: Rebuilding Structure After Sports

One of the biggest shocks after sports is not physical.

It is structural.

For most of your athletic life, someone else built your schedule. Practice times. Lift sessions. Film review. Travel. Meetings. Everything was planned. All you had to do was show up and execute. Discipline was enforced. Accountability was external. Consistency was unavoidable.

Then it stops.

No more mandatory workouts. No one tracking reps. No coach setting the calendar. What used to be enforced discipline becomes optional discipline. That transition quietly breaks a lot of former athletes, not because they lack work ethic, but because the system that supported it disappears.

From Mandatory Workouts to Optional Discipline

In sports, discipline is built into the environment.

Miss practice and there are consequences. Skip workouts and playing time disappears. The structure forces consistency even on days when motivation is low. You do not debate whether to train. You train because it is required.

In the real world, no one blows the whistle.

You can skip workouts.

Delay saving.

Ignore budgeting.

Push decisions to tomorrow.

Nothing happens immediately. That is the danger.

In basketball terms, this is open gym without a coach. Some players still work. Many drift. Effort drops unless structure replaces enforcement. Talent alone does not carry habits forward.

Optional discipline is harder than mandatory discipline. It requires internal accountability, not external pressure.

How Lack of Structure Quietly Breaks Financial Habits

When structure disappears, good habits erode quietly.

Saving becomes inconsistent.

Bills get paid late.

Budgets turn into loose guidelines.

Long-term goals fade into background noise.

There is no dramatic failure. No clear moment where everything breaks. Just slow drift.

Athletes are used to accountability. When it disappears, discipline often disappears with it unless something replaces it. Financial habits suffer first because the consequences feel distant. Skipping a workout feels immediate. Skipping a savings contribution does not.

Over time, that distance compounds into missed progress and unnecessary stress.

Why Motivation Is Not Enough

Many former athletes assume motivation will carry them.

It rarely does.

Motivation fluctuates. Energy rises and falls. Life gets busy. Without structure, motivation becomes unreliable. The days you need discipline most are the days motivation is lowest.

In basketball terms, motivation is adrenaline. It helps in short bursts. Structure wins seasons.

Discipline must be system-driven, not feeling-driven.

Replacing Practice Schedules With Personal Systems

Structure does not disappear after sports.

It has to be rebuilt.

That means creating systems that remove daily decision-making and enforce consistency even when you do not feel like it.

Automatic transfers for savings and investing.

Scheduled financial check-ins.

Calendar reminders for bills and reviews.

Rules that define actions in advance.

In basketball terms, this is self-coached training.

You set your own workouts.

You decide the schedule.

You hold yourself accountable.

The goal is not perfection.

The goal is rhythm.

Rhythm replaces chaos. Systems replace motivation. Consistency returns when structure returns.

Discipline Becomes Internal

After sports, discipline changes location.

It moves from the environment to the individual.

No one is watching.

No one is checking attendance.

No one is tracking effort.

That does not mean discipline matters less. It matters more.

Those who rebuild structure early protect their future. Those who assume habits will carry themselves forward often look up years later wondering where momentum went.

Internal discipline is harder to build, but it lasts longer.

A Coach's Perspective

A coach would be blunt.

Nobody is coming to save you.

Discipline is a choice now.

Build your own structure.

Do not drift.

Freedom without structure is not freedom. It is exposure.

Great players succeed because they respond to structure. Great professionals succeed because they create it.

Game Situations and Decision Points

These moments reveal whether structure exists.

You have flexibility. Do you use it intentionally or waste it?

You miss a habit. Do you reset immediately or let it slide?

No one is watching. Do you still show up?

Outcomes follow structure. Structure determines consistency. Consistency determines results.

Athlete Habits and Financial Parallels

Athletes rely on external accountability.

Financially, that leads to inconsistency.

Athletes underestimate drift.

Financially, that leads to lost progress.

Athletes avoid systems because they feel restrictive.

Financially, that leads to chaos.

The same habits that shorten careers create stress after sports.

Winning the Transition

Rebuilding structure is one of the most important skills after sports.

Systems replace coaches.

Calendars replace practice plans.

Rules replace whistles.

Those who succeed financially after sports are not more motivated. They are more structured. They understand that discipline without structure does not last.

The transition is not about doing more.

It is about building systems that make the right actions automatic.

Athlete Takeaways

Structure disappears after sports.

Optional discipline is harder than enforced discipline.

Lack of structure quietly erodes financial habits.

Motivation fades. Systems last.

Build structure or drift.

The whistle may be gone.

Discipline still decides the outcome.

Chapter 27: From Teammates to Coworkers

Playing Without a Scoreboard: Adapting to the Workplace After Sports

Leaving sports does not just change what you do.

It changes how people work together.

Athletes are raised in environments built on clarity. Roles are defined. Authority is visible. Feedback is direct. Performance is measured. You know who is in charge, what is expected, and how success is judged. When you transition into the workplace, that clarity often disappears, and the culture can feel confusing, political, or frustrating.

This adjustment affects more than job satisfaction. It affects confidence, income growth, and long-term career stability. Many former athletes struggle not because they lack ability, but because they are operating in a system that plays by different rules.

Why the Workplace Feels Foreign After Sports

Sports environments are honest.

If you play well, you play more. If you do not, you sit. Effort is visible. Results are measurable. Expectations are clear. You always know where you stand.

Workplaces rarely function this way.

Performance metrics are often vague. Feedback may be delayed or softened. Promotions are not always tied directly to output. Visibility, timing, and relationships play a much larger role than most athletes expect.

For someone raised on objective evaluation, this can feel disorienting.

In basketball terms, this is playing without a scoreboard.

The game is still happening, but the signals are harder to read. You do not always know whether you are winning or losing until much later. That uncertainty can create frustration and self-doubt if you are not prepared for it.

Authority Without Coaches

In sports, authority is obvious.

Coaches set the plan. Captains lead on the floor. Accountability is enforced immediately. If something goes wrong, responsibility is clear.

In many workplaces, authority is less visible and more political.

Managers may avoid confrontation. Decisions may be influenced by people without formal titles. Power can live in relationships rather than org charts. Understanding who actually makes decisions matters more than understanding job titles.

Former athletes often struggle here because they wait for direction that never comes. They expect clarity to be delivered the way it was in sports. In reality, clarity often has to be requested or created.

In basketball terms, this is running an offense without a coach calling every set. You have to read the floor and make decisions in real time.

Feedback Without Film

Athletes are trained through feedback.

You watch film. You see mistakes. Corrections are immediate and specific. Improvement is tied directly to what you see.

In the workplace, feedback is often delayed, indirect, or avoided entirely.

Many managers do not enjoy difficult conversations. As a result, you may not know you are struggling until consequences show up in reviews, compensation decisions, or missed opportunities.

In basketball terms, this is playing without film review.

If you want feedback, you usually have to ask for it. If you want clarity, you have to seek it out. Self-evaluation becomes critical. Waiting to be corrected is risky when signals are subtle.

Former athletes who adapt learn to request feedback regularly and professionally. They do not assume silence means success.

Politics, Ambiguity, and Unwritten Rules

Workplaces include politics.

Relationships matter. Perception matters. Timing matters. These realities feel uncomfortable to athletes who expect effort and results to speak for themselves.

Ignoring politics does not make them disappear. It simply removes your ability to navigate them.

Understanding workplace dynamics does not mean compromising values. It means understanding the environment you are operating in so you can protect opportunity and income.

In basketball terms, this is understanding officiating and game flow. You may not like every call, but you adjust so you can still compete effectively.

Awareness beats frustration.

How This Impacts Income Growth and Career Stability

Confusion slows progress.

Unclear expectations lead to missed opportunities. Poor communication stalls advancement. Frustration builds when effort does not translate into recognition. Many former athletes respond by disengaging or changing jobs too frequently.

Job hopping without strategy disrupts momentum, benefits, and long-term growth. Disengagement reduces visibility and leverage.

Former athletes who adapt tend to grow faster.

They ask questions.

They seek clarity.

They build relationships.

They advocate for themselves professionally.

They treat career development the same way they treated skill development in sports. Intentionally.

Those who do not adapt often feel stuck, overlooked, or undervalued despite working hard.

Ownership Replaces Structure

In sports, structure is provided.

In the workplace, structure is optional.

That means responsibility shifts to you.

You must define goals.

You must request feedback.

You must communicate expectations.

You must track progress.

Waiting for structure that never arrives leads to stagnation. Taking ownership restores momentum.

In basketball terms, this is becoming a floor general. You still play within the system, but you take responsibility for directing your own growth.

A Coach's Perspective

A coach would be direct.

Learn the system.

Communicate clearly.

Ask for feedback.

Take ownership.

You are still responsible for your development, even when no one is tracking it for you.

Game Situations and Decision Points

These moments define outcomes.

You are unsure what matters. Do you ask for clarity or guess and hope?

You want advancement. Do you wait to be noticed or advocate professionally?

You feel frustrated. Do you disengage or adapt your approach?

Awareness changes outcomes. Silence rarely helps.

Athlete Habits and Financial Parallels

Athletes wait for direction.

Financially, that stalls income growth.

Athletes avoid politics entirely.

Financially, that limits opportunity.

Athletes expect fairness to be automatic.

Financially, that leads to frustration instead of progress.

The same habits that cost playing time can cost earning power.

Winning in a Different System

The workplace is not the locker room.

The rules are different. Feedback is quieter. Structure is looser. But success is still possible for former athletes who adapt without losing discipline.

Those who thrive translate work ethic into communication, awareness, and ownership. They learn the system instead of fighting it. They protect their income by staying relevant, visible, and adaptable.

Athlete Takeaways

The workplace lacks the clarity of sports.

Authority and feedback are less obvious.

Politics and perception matter.

Communication protects income growth.

Adaptation builds career stability.

The game changed.

Your discipline still applies.

Chapter 28: When No One Is Watching Anymore

When No One Is Watching: The Discipline Gap After Sports

One of the hardest transitions after sports happens quietly.

There is no crowd.

No coach.

No scoreboard.

Accountability disappears, and with it, the pressure that once kept habits sharp. Many former athletes struggle not because they lost discipline, but because the environment that enforced it is gone. What once felt automatic now requires intention.

This gap catches people off guard.

When Accountability Disappears

In sports, accountability is constant.

Miss a workout and it is noticed. Skip preparation and it shows on the court. Film does not lie. Coaches do not guess. Structure forces discipline whether you feel motivated or not.

After sports, accountability becomes internal.

You can skip saving.

Delay planning.

Ignore habits.

Nothing happens immediately.

That delay is dangerous.

In basketball terms, this is playing pickup without keeping score. The game still happens, but intensity drops unless you bring it yourself. Without consequences, effort becomes optional. Over time, optional effort becomes inconsistent effort.

Why Former Athletes Drift Without Pressure

Pressure sharpens focus.

Deadlines matter. Playing time is earned. Consequences are clear. When pressure disappears, comfort quietly fills the space it leaves behind.

Netflix replaces workouts.

Spending replaces saving.

Short-term relief replaces long-term progress.

This is not laziness. It is human behavior.

Former athletes are conditioned to respond to external pressure. When that pressure disappears, many struggle to generate urgency on their own. The result is not failure. It is drift.

Drift feels harmless in the moment. Over time, it compounds.

Comfort Versus Growth Decisions

Every meaningful decision lives somewhere between comfort and growth.

Comfort feels good now.

Growth feels uncomfortable now but pays off later.

In basketball terms, comfort is settling for a contested jumper early in the shot clock. Growth is running the offense, moving the ball, and waiting for a better look.

Money mistakes often come from choosing comfort repeatedly.

Ordering out instead of planning.

Spending instead of saving.

Avoiding planning because it feels stressful.

None of these choices hurt immediately. That is why they are easy to repeat. The cost shows up years later, when options feel limited and stress increases.

Growth decisions rarely feel urgent.

They feel optional.

Until they are not.

Why Grind Culture Does Not Translate

Many former athletes try to replace structure with intensity.

They grind.

They push harder.

They try to recreate the pressure they once lived under.

That approach rarely works long term.

Adult life does not reward effort alone. It rewards consistency, systems, and results. Without structure, grind culture leads to burnout, frustration, and eventually disengagement.

In sports, grind is scheduled.

In life, grind without systems is chaos.

The goal is not constant intensity.

The goal is sustainable discipline.

Money Has Delayed Feedback

One of the hardest adjustments after sports is delayed feedback.

In basketball, mistakes show up immediately. Miss an assignment and the other team scores. Skip conditioning and you feel it late in the game.

Money works differently.

Overspending today creates stress years later.

Skipping saving now limits options later.

Poor decisions compound quietly.

In basketball terms, this is blowing assignments in the first quarter that cost you in the fourth. You do not feel the damage right away, but it accumulates.

Delayed feedback makes discipline harder because the connection between action and consequence is less obvious. That is why systems matter.

Replacing External Pressure With Internal Systems

When external accountability disappears, it must be replaced.

Not with motivation.

With systems.

Automatic savings.

Scheduled reviews.

Clear rules for spending and planning.

Non-negotiable habits.

These systems recreate pressure without relying on emotion.

In basketball terms, this is self-coached training. No one is making you show up. You do it because you know what happens if you do not. Systems carry you on days motivation disappears.

Discipline becomes a choice.

Then it becomes a habit.

Then it becomes identity.

A Coach's Perspective

A coach would be honest.

Nobody is watching now.

That does not mean it does not matter.

Discipline is your responsibility.

Choose growth over comfort.

Great players are not defined by how they perform under pressure alone. They are defined by what they do when pressure is absent.

Game Situations and Decision Points

These moments shape outcomes.

You are tired. Do you choose comfort or discipline?

No one notices. Do you show up anyway?

The payoff feels far away. Do you stay consistent or drift?

What you do when no one is watching defines results.

Athlete Habits and Financial Parallels

Athletes rely on pressure.

Financially, that leads to drift.

Athletes chase comfort.

Financially, that leads to overspending.

Athletes confuse grind with progress.

Financially, that leads to burnout.

The same habits that shorten careers create stress later in life.

Winning Without an Audience

Discipline without an audience is harder.

It is also more powerful.

The habits you maintain privately shape the results you see publicly. Former athletes who rebuild discipline internally do not rely on motivation or pressure. They rely on systems, consistency, and awareness.

They do not wait to feel ready.

They do not wait to be watched.

They show up anyway.

Athlete Takeaways

Accountability disappears after sports.

Discipline must become internal.

Comfort choices compound into problems.

Sustainable systems beat grind culture.

What you do when no one is watching matters most.

The crowd is gone.

The work still counts.

Chapter 29: Redefining Winning After the Uniform Comes Off

Redefining the Scoreboard: Winning Without a Uniform

For most of your life, winning was clearly defined.

Points. Minutes. Championships. Depth charts. Everything had a metric. You knew if you were improving because the scoreboard told you. Effort showed up in playing time. Progress showed up in results. Feedback was constant.

Then the uniform comes off.

The metrics disappear, but the competitive instinct does not. Many former athletes struggle not because they stopped wanting to win, but because they no longer know how winning is measured. What used to be about mastery quietly turns into comparison.

That shift changes everything.

Why Status Replaces Performance

Sports reward performance.

Life often rewards appearance.

Without a scoreboard, success becomes harder to measure. So people default to what is visible. Income. Titles. Houses. Cars. Job labels. These become stand-ins for progress because they are easy to compare and easy to show.

In basketball terms, this is playing for the crowd instead of running the offense.

Status provides quick validation. It feels like proof. Performance takes longer and is harder to explain. Over time, chasing status replaces chasing growth, even though it rarely produces the same satisfaction.

Former athletes are especially vulnerable to this trap because they are wired to compete. When the game changes and the rules are unclear, comparison fills the gap.

Income Matters, but It Is Not the Finish Line

Income matters.

It creates stability. It reduces stress. It buys flexibility and options. Ignoring income entirely is unrealistic and irresponsible. But income alone does not create fulfillment.

Many former athletes hit income milestones and still feel restless. The competition is gone. The structure is gone. The sense of purpose feels muted. The numbers look good, but something feels off.

In basketball terms, this is scoring points on a losing team.

The stat line looks impressive. The experience does not. Fulfillment comes from alignment, growth, contribution, and control over time. Income supports those things. It does not replace them.

When income becomes the only scoreboard, it eventually disappoints.

Titles, Houses, Cars, and the Comparison Trap

Comparison is constant.

Social media amplifies it. Former teammates become measuring sticks. Someone else's promotion, purchase, or lifestyle becomes a silent benchmark. Lifestyle inflation starts to masquerade as success.

Chasing symbols creates pressure that never ends. There is always someone with more. More money. More recognition. More visibility.

In basketball terms, this is chasing highlight reels instead of winning games.

Highlights feel good in the moment. Championships require discipline, patience, and teamwork. Comparison pulls attention away from progress and toward noise. It distorts decision-making and encourages spending, career moves, and commitments that do not align with what actually matters.

Comparison is a poor coach.

What Success Looks Like in Your 30s and 40s

Success evolves.

In your 30s and 40s, winning often looks quieter than it did in your 20s. It looks like flexibility. Health. Control over your schedule. Time with people who matter. Financial stability without constant anxiety.

It looks like optionality instead of urgency.

These wins do not show up on a stat sheet. They show up in how you feel on Monday mornings. In how you sleep. In how much margin you have when life changes.

Former athletes who redefine success early make better decisions. They stop chasing symbols that no longer fit. Those who do not often feel stuck competing in a game they no longer enjoy.

Building a New Scoreboard

If you want to win, you need metrics.

You cannot win a game if you do not know the score.

After sports, you have to build a new scoreboard intentionally. One that reflects the life you want, not the life that looks impressive to others.

New metrics might include:

Peace of mind.

Control over your schedule.

Alignment with your values.

Progress toward long-term goals.

Health and energy.

In basketball terms, this is redefining the game you are playing.

You are no longer competing for minutes. You are competing for quality of life. That requires different measurements and different strategies.

Visibility Versus Fulfillment

Visibility feels like winning because it is public.

Fulfillment feels quieter because it is internal.

Former athletes often confuse the two because sports reward visibility. After sports, that equation flips. The most meaningful wins are rarely the most visible ones.

Building a life that fits you requires resisting the urge to explain it to everyone else. That resistance is uncomfortable at first. Over time, it becomes freeing.

A Coach's Perspective

A coach would reframe the conversation.

Define your game.

Measure what matters.

Stop playing for the crowd.

Win on your terms.

Great players adjust when the game changes. They do not cling to old rules that no longer apply.

Game Situations and Decision Points

These moments reveal what scoreboard you are using.

You see someone else's success. Do you compare or stay focused?

You hit a goal. Do you ask what is next, or what actually matters?

You feel pressure to upgrade. Do you chase status or protect alignment?

The scoreboard you choose changes every decision that follows.

Athlete Habits and Financial Parallels

Athletes chase validation.

Financially, that leads to overspending.

Athletes avoid introspection.

Financially, that leads to misaligned goals.

Athletes confuse winning with visibility.

Financially, that leads to regret.

The habits that helped you win before need refinement to help you win now.

Winning the Long Game

Redefining winning is not lowering standards.

It is raising them.

It means choosing fulfillment over comparison. Alignment over appearance. Sustainability over short-term validation. When success matches who you are and how you want to live, the game becomes meaningful again.

You stop chasing noise.

You start building something that lasts.

Athlete Takeaways

Status is not the same as success.

Income supports fulfillment but does not replace it.

Comparison distorts decision-making.

Success evolves with life stages.

Build a new scoreboard that reflects what matters.

The uniform is gone.

The competition is still there.

Chapter 30: Staying Connected Without Living in the Past

Staying Connected Without Living in the Past

One of the quiet losses after sports is not competition.

It is connection.

The locker room disappears. Daily contact fades. Shared struggle is replaced by individual schedules. Many former athletes underestimate how much of their identity was built around being part of a team until it is gone.

That loss does not announce itself.

It shows up slowly.

Staying connected matters.

Living in the past does not.

Why Community Matters After Sports

Athletes thrive in community.

They perform better with accountability, shared goals, and support. The locker room provides structure without effort. You show up, and connection is built into the day. After sports, that structure disappears unless it is rebuilt intentionally.

Community does not happen by accident anymore.

It has to be chosen.

New locker rooms exist.

Work teams.

Professional organizations.

Volunteer groups.

Faith communities.

Peer networks.

Alumni circles.

These spaces provide accountability, perspective, and belonging. They replace isolation with shared purpose.

Mentorship matters too.

Learning from people a few steps ahead shortens the learning curve. Mentors provide context when the new environment feels confusing. They normalize the transition and offer perspective that cannot be found alone.

In basketball terms, this is finding a new team that fits the next phase of your career.

Why Isolation Hits Former Athletes Hard

Isolation is dangerous because it is subtle.

Former athletes go from constant interaction to quiet independence almost overnight. The silence feels like freedom at first. Over time, it becomes disorienting.

Without teammates, feedback disappears.

Without feedback, perspective narrows.

Without perspective, mistakes repeat.

In basketball terms, this is playing without communication. Missed assignments multiply. Nobody calls out screens. The game falls apart quietly.

Isolation often disguises itself as productivity. Overworking. Staying busy. Filling time without connection. On the surface, it looks like discipline. Underneath, motivation fades and clarity suffers.

Former athletes are wired for team environments. Removing that environment without replacement creates a vacuum.

Finding Purpose Without the Team

Purpose does not disappear when the team does.

It changes.

Competition is replaced by contribution. Wins are replaced by impact. Applause is replaced by responsibility. Many former athletes struggle because they search for the exact feeling sports gave them instead of building something new.

That feeling rarely returns in the same form.

In basketball terms, this is refusing to adjust your role when the lineup changes. The game continues, but your contribution looks different.

Leadership becomes purpose.

Teaching becomes purpose.

Building becomes purpose.

Mentoring becomes purpose.

Purpose comes from impact, not applause. It shows up when your actions matter to others, even if nobody is keeping score.

Healthy Nostalgia Versus Being Stuck

Remembering your playing days is normal.

Living there is not.

Healthy nostalgia honors the past without letting it define the future. It allows gratitude without attachment. Being stuck shows up when identity stops evolving.

You can usually hear it.

Every story ends with what you used to do.

Every comparison points backward.

Every sense of worth is tied to a former version of yourself.

In basketball terms, this is replaying old highlights instead of preparing for the next game. The memories stay sharp, but progress stalls.

The past should inform you.

It should not trap you.

Creating a Forward-Looking Identity

Identity has to move forward.

You are not an athlete who used to play.

You are a person who learned discipline, resilience, teamwork, and accountability through sports.

Those traits still matter.

They just apply differently.

In basketball terms, this is transferring skills to a new system. The court looks different. The pace changes. The fundamentals still work.

Former athletes who thrive stop asking, "Who was I?"

They start asking, "Who am I becoming?"

That shift changes everything.

Connection Requires Intentional Effort

After sports, connection is no longer automatic.

You have to reach out.

You have to show up.

You have to stay involved even when it feels uncomfortable.

Waiting for community to find you rarely works. Building it requires initiative, humility, and consistency. The same traits that made you valuable on a team apply here.

Connection is not about replacing the locker room.

It is about building something that fits your life now.

A Coach's Perspective

A coach would challenge you directly.

Honor the past.

Build the present.

Invest in the future.

Keep growing.

Stagnation is the real loss, not the end of competition.

Growth requires movement. Movement requires connection.

Game Situations and Decision Points

These moments define direction.

You feel disconnected. Do you isolate or seek community?

You miss the team. Do you rebuild structure or live in memory?

You define yourself by the past. Do you evolve or stay stuck?

Connection shapes identity. Identity shapes behavior. Behavior shapes outcomes.

Athlete Habits and Financial Parallels

Athletes cling to past identity.

Financially, that leads to stagnation.

Athletes isolate.

Financially, that leads to poor decisions and limited perspective.

Athletes avoid change.

Financially, that limits opportunity and growth.

The same habits that once protected identity can eventually restrict it.

Winning in a New Way

Staying connected does not mean staying the same.

Growth requires new relationships, new roles, and new purpose. Former athletes who build forward-looking identity thrive because they keep learning, contributing, and connecting.

The game does not end.

It changes.

When you accept that, connection returns in new forms and meaning deepens.

Athlete Takeaways

Community matters long after competition ends.

Isolation quietly erodes motivation and clarity.

Purpose evolves beyond the team.

Honor the past without living in it.

Build a forward-looking identity and keep moving forward.

The locker room is gone.

You are still part of a team.

Glossary of Basketball and Financial Terms

This glossary connects key financial concepts to familiar ideas from **basketball**, making money easier to understand through the language, structure, spacing, and discipline athletes already know.

Asset Allocation

Financial Definition:

How money is divided among different investment types such as stocks, bonds, and cash to balance risk and return.

Basketball Comparison:

How scoring, defense, rebounding, and pace are balanced within a game plan. Overloading one area without balance leads to breakdowns.

Assets

Financial Definition:

Things you own that have value, such as cash, investments, real estate, or retirement accounts.

Basketball Comparison:

Your strengths as a player. Shooting, defense, conditioning, IQ, and experience that contribute to winning.

Bonds

Financial Definition:

Loans made to governments or companies that pay interest and return principal over time.

Basketball Comparison:

Interior defense and rebounding. Not flashy, but essential for stability when the game gets physical.

Budget

Financial Definition:

A plan for how income is allocated toward expenses, savings, and goals.

Basketball Comparison:

The game plan. Without knowing where shots, possessions, and effort are supposed to go, execution falls apart.

Cash Flow

Financial Definition:

Money coming in versus money going out.

Basketball Comparison:

Energy and stamina. Push too hard early without control and you struggle late.

Compounding

Financial Definition:

Earnings that generate additional earnings over time.

Basketball Comparison:

Daily reps and muscle memory. Small improvements stack until the game slows down and execution becomes automatic.

Credit

Financial Definition:

The ability to borrow money with the promise of repayment.

Basketball Comparison:

Trust from the coach. Earned through consistency, lost quickly through mistakes.

Debt

Financial Definition:

Money borrowed that must be repaid, often with interest.

Basketball Comparison:

Extra defensive pressure. Manageable in short stretches, dangerous if it becomes constant.

Diversification

Financial Definition:

Spreading investments across different assets to reduce risk.

Basketball Comparison:

Not relying on one scorer or one lineup to win every game.

Emergency Fund

Financial Definition:

Savings set aside for unexpected expenses.

Basketball Comparison:

A deep bench. You hope you do not need it, but it keeps the team alive when things go wrong.

ETF (Exchange-Traded Fund)

Financial Definition:

A fund that holds many investments and trades like a stock.

Basketball Comparison:

A full rotation instead of isolation basketball. Team-based execution over hero ball.

Fees / Expense Ratios

Financial Definition:

Costs associated with managing investments.

Basketball Comparison:

Unforced turnovers. Small mistakes that quietly swing outcomes.

Growth Investing

Financial Definition:

Investing in companies expected to grow faster than average.

Basketball Comparison:

Up-tempo offense. Higher upside, but it requires discipline to avoid mistakes.

Insurance

Financial Definition:

Protection against financial loss from unexpected events.

Basketball Comparison:

Protective gear and training staff. You do not step on the court without protection when contact is guaranteed.

Liquidity

Financial Definition:

How easily money can be accessed without penalty or delay.

Basketball Comparison:

Floor spacing. The ability to move, adjust, and react under pressure.

Net Worth

Financial Definition:

Assets minus liabilities.

Basketball Comparison:

The scoreboard. Not one highlight, but the final result.

Rebalancing

Financial Definition:

Adjusting investments back to their intended mix over time.

Basketball Comparison:

Mid-game adjustments to restore rhythm and control.

Risk

Financial Definition:

The chance that outcomes differ from expectations, including loss.

Basketball Comparison:

Shot selection. Higher difficulty brings higher reward, but also higher risk.

Roth IRA

Financial Definition:

A retirement account where money grows tax-free if rules are followed.

Basketball Comparison:

Putting in extra work early so the fourth quarter feels easier.

Stocks

Financial Definition:

Ownership shares in a company.

Basketball Comparison:

Primary scorers. They drive results but need support to win consistently.

Tax-Advantaged Accounts

Financial Definition:

Accounts that provide tax benefits, often with rules and restrictions.

Basketball Comparison:

Structured practice systems. Rules exist to maximize performance.

Volatility

Financial Definition:

Short-term ups and downs in market value.

Basketball Comparison:

A scoring run by the opponent. Normal unless you panic and lose composure.

Permanent Loss

Financial Definition:

Money that cannot recover due to poor decisions or panic.

Basketball Comparison:

A technical foul or ejection. Damage caused by losing control.

Total Return

Financial Definition:

Investment return from both price growth and income.

Basketball Comparison:

The full box score. Points, rebounds, assists, defense. Everything matters.

Value Investing

Financial Definition:

Investing in assets believed to be undervalued.

Basketball Comparison:

Fundamentals and execution. Less flash, more consistency.

Yield

Financial Definition:

Income generated from an investment.

Basketball Comparison:

Reliable scoring. Not always spectacular, but dependable.

Final Note

This glossary reinforces one core principle:

Financial success, like success in **basketball**, comes from balance, discipline, timing, and repetition.

That philosophy runs throughout **BasketballMoney101** and continues long after the final buzzer.

Disclaimer

This book is for educational purposes only.

The information provided in *BasketballMoney 101* is intended to help readers understand general financial concepts using basketball-based analogies. It is not individualized financial, investment, tax, legal, or insurance advice.

Every financial situation is different. Your goals, income, family circumstances, risk tolerance, and time horizon are unique. What works for one person may not be appropriate for another.

Not Financial, Investment, or Legal Advice

Nothing in this book should be interpreted as a recommendation to buy, sell, or hold any specific investment, financial product, or strategy.

This book does not replace advice from qualified professionals such as:

- Financial advisors
- Accountants or tax professionals
- Attorneys
- Insurance professionals

Before making financial decisions, readers should consult professionals who can evaluate their individual situation.

No Guarantees or Promises of Results

All investing involves risk, including the possible loss of principal.

Past performance does not guarantee future results. Markets fluctuate. Economic conditions change. Outcomes cannot be predicted or guaranteed.

The examples and scenarios in this book are illustrative only and may not reflect actual results or real-world outcomes.

Tax and Legal Information

Any discussion of taxes, retirement accounts, estate planning, or legal structures is general in nature.

Tax laws and regulations change frequently and vary by jurisdiction. Legal requirements differ based on location and personal circumstances.

Readers should seek personalized tax or legal advice before acting on any information related to these topics.

Athlete and Career Considerations

This book discusses financial topics as they relate to athletes and former athletes, including career transitions, income variability, and post-sport planning.

It does not provide career placement services, employment advice, or guarantees related to income, compensation, endorsements, NIL opportunities, or career success.

Use of Analogies

Basketball and sports analogies are used to make financial concepts easier to understand.

These analogies are educational tools only and should not be interpreted literally. Financial decisions require analysis beyond analogy and comparison.

Personal Responsibility

By reading this book, you acknowledge that:

- You are responsible for your own financial decisions
- You understand that financial outcomes involve uncertainty
- You agree to seek appropriate professional guidance when needed

Education improves decision-making, but responsibility remains with the individual.

Contact Information

If you would like to learn more about the concepts discussed in this book or explore additional educational resources, **Pat Brown** can be found through public platforms including LinkedIn, Twitter, and via Google search.

For questions specifically related to **BasketballMoney101**, you may contact Pat Brown at:

info@basketballmoney101.com

Final Reminder

Financial success is built over time through discipline, planning, and consistency.

This book provides a framework, not a guarantee.

Use it as a guide, not a substitute for professional advice.

Pat Brown OLB, University of Kansas

Made in the USA
Monee, IL
04 November 2026

67387579R00128